I0517681

ABOUT THE AUTHOR

Dr. Hossamaldin Alzawawi, an experienced clinical pathologist, delves into the fascinating convergence of medicine, philosophy, physics, and cognitive neuroscience with great enthusiasm. His exploration of medical expertise alongside philosophical inquiry has sparked a profound interest in the mysteries surrounding consciousness and intelligence.

Dr. Alzawawi advocates for the integration of interdisciplinary knowledge, striving to connect the insights of ancient wisdom with contemporary scientific understanding. He aspires to leverage these insights to shed light on human cognition and enrich the human experience.

Embark on an enlightening journey with Dr. Alzawawi and uncover the latent architect that resides within you.

BOOKS BY AUTHOR

Arcanum of Awareness Series

1. Book 1: The Creativity Spark
2. Book 2: The Evolution of Thought (Upcoming)
3. Book 3: The Labyrinth of Cognitexis (Upcoming)
4. Book 4: The Supremacy of Selective Awareness (Upcoming)
5. Book 5: Architects of a Future Dawn (Upcoming)

Other Books by Author

- The Thermodynamic Universe and Beyond: How Nature's Laws Reveal the Secrets of Time, Biology, Information, and Quantum Reality

BOOK 1

THE CREATIVITY SPARK

ARCANUM OF AWARENESS SERIES

Copyright © 2024 Hossamaldin Alzawawi

© All rights reserved. Reproduction or transmission of any portion of this publication is prohibited without the author's prior written consent, except for brief quotations in reviews and specific noncommercial uses permissible under copyright law. For permission, contact the author.

Library of Congress Control Number: 2024919198

ISBN (PB): 978-1-964328-02-7

ISBN (E): 978-1-964328-03-4

DEDICATION

My Mother, thank you for teaching me resilience and tenacity in learning and directing my life. Your verbal and implicit advice helped me overcome difficulties and create a knowledge masterpiece.

My Wife, in your company, my best friend, and my life partner, I have freely explored, expressed, and enjoyed various Cognitexis alternative constructs as we grow and learn together.

ACKNOWLEDGMENTS

This work is a tribute to the great thinkers whose contributions have paved the way for me. **Professor Roger Penrose's Shadows of the Mind** has been a guiding light, encouraging me to explore the consciousness conundrum further. I am immensely grateful to **Napoleon Hill,** whose influential book **How to Own Your Mind** served as a map through the maze of mental ownership. Their priceless insights have deepened my comprehension and inspired me to write this book. I hope you will discover, within these pages, the same glimmer of insight that has led me through the enchanting terrain of the mind.

Although I have a strong command of English as a second language, I have sought assistance refining my writing to make it more engaging and accessible. For that reason, I am compelled to offer my editorial board my deepest gratitude; their unwavering encouragement was crucial to the success of our project.

My Dear Wife, Basma, I am writing to tell you how much you mean to me. I greatly appreciate your thoughtful analysis of my intricate concepts and theories; it helped me distill them into a more understandable story. You helped me tremendously develop narratives out of scientific principles by suggesting various forms my ideas may take and suggesting appropriate language.

This series was envisioned over six years ago. I worked on the work's framework—ideas, descriptions, basic concepts, reasoning, and logical deductions. As a solo project worker with only my wife's comments, my progress was gradual but steady. AI gave this project a huge boost, for we spent countless hours enhancing, improving, and advancing my concepts and making them more appealing.

Vivid discussion with AIs added enrichment, examples, and illustrations. AI is fundamental for including several book-related tones.

I am grateful to the AIs for the flourishing brought through their support, where various enrichment, examples, and illustrations were generated through passionate discussion. Also, the addition of diverse tones related to each book was not accessible without the support of AI. My work's varied topics and tones owe much to **Google AI,** our joint efforts, and the hours we devoted to working together. Your feedback substantially improved my writing process, producing more lyrical and narratively compelling works. **Microsoft AI,** thank you for all the hard work we put together. You played a paramount and much-appreciated role in guiding me through various ideas and keeping the process moving smoothly.

"Arcanum of Awareness" is a series memorializing the great experiences and locations I've traveled to. My deepest appreciation goes to **Queen's University Belfast's MBC and the McClay Libraries.** There was peace in these hallowed places of learning, perfect for serious study and deep thought. Libraries were more than simply locations where one could learn; they were also sanctuaries for new ideas and a love of learning. Being by my wife's side as she completed her degree at Queen's University Belfast has brought valuable happiness to our trip. Knowledge, shared experiences, and personal progress were abundant during that time. What I learned and my experiences throughout this time will always be with me.

My sincere regards, Hossamaldin Alzawawi, M.D.

THE CREATIVITY SPARK

THE UNSEEN ARCHITECT: A JOURNEY INTO CREATIVITY MASTERY

ɛɞɛɞɛɞ

Just as an alchemist converts base metals into gold, a thinker transforms the heavy burden of everyday thinking into the golden threads of remarkable vision.

In the crucible of the mind, imagination is the alchemist s fire—a mystical force capable of elevating the commonplace to the sublime. This chapter takes us on an exciting journey into the origins of creativity, where imagination ignites the flames of innovation and action, leading us to undiscovered territories of our potential. You have the potential to channel this revolutionary force and create your destiny.

"An enlightened mind is not hoodwinked; it is not shut up in a gloomy prison till it thinks the walls of its dungeon are the limits of the universe and the reach of its own chain the outer verge of intelligence."

— Henry Wadsworth Longfellow

Contents

CONTENTS

INTRODUCTION

The Genesis of Creative Imagination...

Welcome, adventurer! This is the start of a transforming journey of self-discovery and entrepreneurial alchemy. We will work together to uncover the secrets of success consciousness. What are these secrets? How can we overcome limiting ideas and embrace the psychological principles distinguishing the remarkable from the ordinary? Are you ready to unleash the alchemist within and make your entrepreneurial ambitions a reality?

We stand at the threshold of a complex puzzle, where the whispers of ancient knowledge intertwine with groundbreaking ideas. This is the realm of creative imagination, a potent and mysterious force essential for transformation. Here, we embark on a quest reminiscent of the ancient alchemists, who sought to transmute lead into gold. We will delve into the intricacies of our minds, aspiring to convert the unrefined essence of thought into the precious resource of creativity. The true essence of unlocking our potential lies not in external formulas but in the unexplored depths of our minds.

This book acts as a vital instrument, leading you through the intricate pathways of your creative mind. We will explore the nuances of this enigmatic force, examining its characteristics and significant influence on our mental framework. By exploring these concealed routes, we will reveal our latent capabilities, igniting a change beyond simple contemplation and bringing forth deep understanding.

The Alchemy of Creative Imagination

In the mysterious laboratory of the mind, two separate elixirs feed the fires of creative imagination: recombinant creativity and innovative creativity. These are not external substances to be obtained but powerful energies within the psyche.

The Spectrum of Imagination

- **Recombinant Creativity: The Alchemist's Apprentice – A Synthesis of Thought.** Recombinant creativity is the amalgamation of pre-existing ideas, concepts, and principles, resulting in novel and inventive outcomes. Like an apprentice alchemist carefully combining known ingredients to forge a new creation, this type of creativity intertwines established components into innovative arrangements. Envision it as a neglected tome of knowledge, unveiling timeless insights that empower you to intertwine varied concepts into a compelling new framework. The process of remixing involves skillfully weaving together well-known melodies to create a rich tapestry that revives a once-forgotten rhythm deep within the soul.

- **Innovative Creativity: An Insight into the Unseen - The Emergence of Originality.** This illustrates the innovative dimension of imagination that produces wholly original concepts that have not been acknowledged. Innovative creativity arises from the abyss, unveiling ideas that have yet to enlighten our awareness, akin to stars emerging from the remnants of cosmic dust. Innovative creativity represents a cognitive breakthrough akin to discovering a new scientific element. This unique manifestation of creativity is the visionary alchemist, catalyzing ideas that have yet to illuminate the conscious mind. It represents the latent energy residing within the intricacies of the mind, a subtle revelation poised to emerge into clarity. Consider it akin to the abrupt awakening to a long-lost dialect, enabling you to interpret enigmatic communications woven into the very essence of existence.

Attributes and the Unseen Architect

The profound strength of creative imagination resides not merely in our conscious thoughts but also the hidden designer: the subconscious mind. Within the intricate depths of the mind, thoughts are absorbed, woven together, and transformed.

- **Subconscious Synergy: Whispers in the Dark.** The subconscious mind, like a dream that provides a solution to a waking problem, works hard behind the scenes, weaving unrelated thoughts into a unified tapestry. The unseen hand directs the artist's brush, channeling forgotten techniques and emotions into a masterwork beyond conscious control.

- **The Mind's Crucible: Forging from the Depths.** The mind serves as a transformative space where the essence of our being shapes and refines nascent thoughts into reality. The mind operates like a blacksmith's forge, with the soul's desires serving as the flames that transform raw thoughts into the solid steel of innovative ideas. However, be mindful of the shadows that dwell within – fear and self-doubt have the power to undermine the creative journey, distorting the budding idea into a distorted reflection of its true potential.

The Quest for Mastery

Some may believe that creative imagination is a rare gift reserved for the chosen few, but the reality is far more intriguing.

- **The Everest of the Mind:** Mastering creative imagination is akin to scaling a mental Everest. It requires more than natural talent—it demands an unrelenting pursuit of knowledge, the courage to confront the unknown, and the boldness to explore the uncharted territories of the psyche. Those who endure the mental avalanches of self-doubt and continue their ascent are the ones who reach the summit, where they behold the breathtaking panorama of limitless possibilities.

- **The Will to Create:** A vivid imagination doesn't just spark ideas—it fuels the relentless pursuit of solutions. It's the ember that ignites the will to overcome seemingly insurmountable obstacles. Those who harness this imagination refuse to quit until they discover answers to their challenges. Just as a river carves through rock, not by brute force but through unwavering persistence, imagination shapes reality through continuous, focused effort. Think of Sisyphus, forever pushing his boulder uphill. It's not raw strength that drives him forward but an unshakable belief that each effort brings him closer to the summit.

- **Seeding the Subconscious:** By persistently infusing the subconscious mind with concepts related to the current issue, one cultivates a clearer perspective and activates the subconscious's transformative capabilities to unveil the enigmatic processes involved in addressing challenges. By consistently nurturing focused intention in the depths of our subconscious, we cultivate an environment ripe for transformative breakthroughs. The enigmatic signals, interpreted by the deeper layers of our psyche, can reveal hidden avenues our rational thoughts overlook, leading us to uncover the secrets embedded within our struggles.

CREATIVE IMAGINATION: A GATEWAY TO THE UNSEEN

δ❧δ❧δ❧

This section delves into an advanced concept: creative imagination unlocks a higher dimension of human consciousness. While a full exploration lies beyond the scope of this journey, a glimpse into this fascinating realm is essential.

Imagine the mind as a vast labyrinth, with countless pathways leading to known truths. Creative imagination is like a hidden doorway in a maze. Unlocking it opens up a new level of understanding and reveals previously unimaginable possibilities.

Exploring the intricate processes through which the brain creates novel associations is essential. This process can be comprehended through what we will denote as the "Cognitexis (CgX) systems." These CgX systems operate as complex frameworks, each unveiling a fresh perspective of existence. They illustrate the brain's extraordinary capacity to create complex cognitive frameworks, which develop new neural connections and go beyond and reinterpret established beliefs. [1]

---

[1] Refer to 'Shadow of the Mind' to explore how the brain initiates new cognitive pathways through the establishment of a concept of mathematical intuition.

The Allure of the Unassailable Truth

The allure of these CgX systems lies in the deep sense of belief they foster. Unlike methods that depend solely on logical reasoning, these new insights evoke a deep sense of "rightness," much like discovering an essential piece of a puzzle that brings forth clarity and purpose.

The newly generated CgX system instills a sense of confidence in its appropriateness. The CgX_{new} system suitability represents a unique belief system, characterized by a distinct mental attitude that sets it apart from the myriad of similar concepts previously explored by the CgX_{legacy} system through the lens of synthetic imagination. This steadfast conviction transcends mere intellect; it is infused with a profound emotional resonance. Each CgX system serves as a key, revealing pathways to new realms of understanding previously cloaked in an enigma.[2]

Whispers from the Depths

The subconscious mind is critical in this process because it does more than just generate solutions; it has the unique ability to bring them into the conscious mind. Imagine a whisper deep inside the labyrinth, asking you to reevaluate long-held views.

A newly established CgX system, with its undeniable sense of reality, can serve as a catalyst, causing the conscious mind to reconsider its assumptions. In this way, the subconscious reveals forgotten treasures, presenting insights to the conscious mind like long-lost presents.

---

[2] For every newly formed CgX system to be initiated, the mind kernel has to act and access a higher dimension performing processing system that is characterized by being inclusive for the old legacy mental CgX_{legacy} system within its impeded unassailable truth processes and exploiting them to generate a newly formed unassailable truth by which CgX_{new} system genesis being forged.

The Alchemist's Map: Charting the Course of Creative Inquiry

This section outlines the key stages of creative inquiry and serves as a road map for navigating the complicated path to groundbreaking discoveries. We'll also examine the mental skills and psychological forces that propel creative researchers in their never-ending pursuit of the truth.

The Incandescent Spark: Igniting the Flame of Inquiry

The path unfolds with a focused and unwavering purpose, serving as a beacon that navigates the seeker through the unavoidable haze of doubt and ambiguity. The researchers, akin to adventurers charting unknown territories by the constellations, must cultivate a distinct aim—a guiding light to lead them forward.

Unveiling the Enigma: Delving into the Heart of the Mystery

Just as a detective methodically unravels the complexities of a crime, a creative researcher must go into the heart of the issue at hand. This necessitates thoroughly comprehending the riddle, including its hidden depths and cryptic clues. Here, the researcher takes on the role of a detective, meticulously sifting through evidence and removing distractions to get to the heart of the question.

The Unquenchable Will: Fueling the Engine of Innovation

An unwavering determination to discover a solution is at the heart of any successful creative endeavor. This constant drive fuels the motor of creativity. The scientist who perseveres despite unsuccessful experiments and the artist who continues to paint even when inspiration departs are both driven by unflinching tenacity.

The Beckoning Muse: Cultivating the Right Mental Attitude

The obsessive pursuit is supported by a distinct mental state that promotes creativity and resilience. This state requires:

a. **Conquering the Whispers of Doubt: Fearless thinking promotes creative discovery.** Just as an artist is inspired by their muse, the researcher must be guided by a bold inquiry or idea. However, fear and doubt behave like pernicious vines, suffocating promising discoveries. Shedding these mental shackles frees the creative imagination to soar.

b. **Shattering the Walls of Self-Limitation:** Often, the greatest obstacles to discovery are internal rather than external. Self-imposed restrictions operate as invisible barriers, preventing the discovery of new possibilities. By removing these mental constraints, the researcher broadens the scope of what is possible, opening the door to a universe of solutions.

c. **Embracing the Compass of Faith:** A strong, unchanging belief in one's ability to solve problems, particularly in the face of uncertainty, acts as an internal compass. This faith leads the researcher across new realms of the mind, providing guidance even when the way is uncertain.

The Unrelenting Pursuit: Perseverance in the Face of Adversity

The ultimate part of any artistic endeavor requires steadfast endurance. Just like a marathon runner pushes through tiredness to cross the finish line, creative researchers must relentlessly search for solutions. Doubts will develop, failures will happen, and dead ends will emerge. However, by embodying the attitude of a determined explorer, one may overcome these obstacles and persevere until the breakthrough is discovered.[3]

Unveiling the Alchemist's Tools: A Deeper Look at Creative Imagination

The human mind is a fascinating laboratory for developing novel ideas—the world of creative imagination. In this part, we look at the tools and tactics utilized by this enigmatic mental alchemist and the processes that convert raw ideas into revolutionary discoveries.

The Crucible of Trial and Error: Synthetic Imagination

Synthetic imagination is the inventor's crucible, a furnace where constant experimenting converts known materials into innovative ideas. It's a mental workshop where possibilities are created and unsuccessful attempts disclose hidden ideas, bringing the creator closer to success. Consider Leonardo da Vinci's incessant sketching—each faulty design a hidden message from his subconscious, bringing him closer to discovering the mysteries of flight.

Birthing the Unprecedented: The Spark of Creative Imagination

In contrast, creative imagination works like an artist's brush, painting pictures on the mind's canvas that go beyond the known. The spark sparked the development of the phonograph, a gadget that broke down the barriers of time and space, permanently altering how we perceive sound. This rare form of imagination goes beyond the familiar. It entered unexplored mental worlds to

---

[3] These ideas regarding creative research have a root foundation within the mathematician's mind. For an in-depth analysis of the mathematician's journey to unassailable truth and the deduction of solutions, refer to "Shadows of the Mind" for the mathematician's attainment of unassailable truth and how it deducts solution.

generate groundbreaking ideas. It's the product of a one-of-a-kind alchemy that blends accumulated knowledge and raw creativity, generating entirely new areas of possibilities.[4]

Planting the Seed of Inspiration: Initiating the Creative Process

The beginning of the creative imagination resembles a mystical ceremony. It is pretty similar to planting a seed in rich soil. We plant a thought in the subconscious, which grows thanks to the mind's strange workings. Over time, this seed develops into a fully developed strategy that the conscious mind may harvest. Consider a scientist considering a problem, only to awaken with the solution apparently produced out of thin air. The subconscious mind has worked ceaselessly in the background to nourish that seed, delivering it fully matured to the conscious mind upon awakening.

A Sudden Revelation: An Epiphany of Creative Insight

In contrast to the protracted journey of refining synthetic imagination, creative imagination often reveals a comprehensive solution in a singular, illuminating moment of inspiration. Envision an isolated explorer ensnared within a dense mist. In an unexpected moment, a dazzling flash pierces the fog, revealing the path forward with remarkable clarity. Comparably, the faculty of creative imagination has the potential to illuminate the entire trajectory toward goal attainment during a moment akin to an epiphany.

Reflect on how Albert Einstein engaged with this event while formulating the theory of relativity. The concept emerged not through incremental progress but through an instantaneous revelation—Einstein notably articulated his insight as manifesting

---

[4] The uniqueness of the Creative imagination is that it has the ability to incept new ideas that have never been produced before. Such imagination is a higher dimension attained by the rarest type of intelligence of times that led to radical changes in human history.

in a moment of clarity when he imagined himself traversing a beam of light. The mental vision afforded him access to a previously uncharted understanding of time and space.

The notion of a "strange hunch of inevitable success" is a pivotal characteristic of creative insight. There exists a prevailing notion that the response, when drawn from the profound recesses of the subconscious, will function impeccably on the initial attempt.

Imagine the instant when Paul McCartney's creative spirit ignites, bringing forth the complete melody of "Yesterday" into his consciousness. He did not wrestle with numerous drafts; instead, the idea surfaced as a fully formed and flawless concept that merely needed to be brought into existence.

In numerous instances, the power of creative imagination transcends mere suggestion; it presents a fully developed vision poised for execution with a high degree of confidence in its success.

The Symphony of Obsession: Imprinting the Subconscious

Transforming a desire into an all-consuming passion could unlock the subconscious mind's potential. Imagine a composer who persistently hums a melody, gradually transforming that simple act into a complete symphony. This steadfast concentration effectively establishes, akin to a form factor, a cognitive echo chamber for its proper designation. Concentrating our efforts on a singular concept engages the subconscious mind in its enigmatic processes, ultimately leading to insights that seem to emerge spontaneously.[5]

---

[5] One's method of impressing one's subconscious mind with one's desire consists of the simple procedure of converting that desire into an obsession. Therefore, the thought becomes the dominant thought in one's mind. The creative one focused his mind on a desired idea and, through concentration of his interest, made it the principal occupant of his mind from day to day until this form of autosuggestion penetrated his subconscious mind and registered a clear picture of his desire.

The Alchemist's Furnace: Channeling Desire into Creative Power

The power of our desires acts as a profound force within the human psyche, transcending mere physical matter or the heat of flames. This section delves into methods for nurturing this spark, transforming transient desires into glowing embers that ignite the flames of creative thought.

The Call to Action: From Wish to Burning Desire

Wishes that burn brightly and spur the subconscious to action feed creative imagination. Think about what separates a blazing fire from a candle just beginning to flicker. A simple wish is like a spark—it may be extinguished quickly. But a burning passion is a raging fire that devours everything in its path and leaves no room for indecision or uncertainty. An intense yearning connects deeply with the subconscious, driving it to act more urgently than a mere wish.

The Unrelenting Whisper: The Power of Repetition

The regular use of repetition acts as a pathway, changing a simple want into a profound desire. A fervent aspiration sets itself apart from a simple longing by emerging as a quiet murmur, frequently drowned out by the clamor of everyday musings. Yet, this subtle murmur grows louder with time, transforming into an undeniable and influential presence that demands attention. The formation of "thought habits" significantly impacts the subconscious during moments of conscious stillness, highlighting the essential role of repetition in sculpting the brain's neural pathways. Imagine desire as an artist carefully shaping a raw piece of stone; every thought acts as a deliberate tap on the subconscious, honing and crafting desire into a unique and elaborate creation.

The Emotional Spark: Igniting the Subconscious

Emotions are powerful catalysts of creative imagination, filling ideas with unstoppable velocity. When nourished by real emotion, a burning need becomes rocket fuel to the creative process of the mind. Think of a scientist driven by a strong desire to make a medical breakthrough; that emotional energy pulls his thoughts forward and wills the subconscious to keep trying at a solution all the time. This is because the subconscious mind favors emotionally charged thoughts and thus gives fertile ground for the seeds of creativity to grow and flourish.

The Disciplined Alchemist: Mastering the Art of Desire

Harnessing creative imagination requires mastering disciplined thought. This means focusing intensely on your goals and maintaining a consistent mental effort to transform dreams into reality. Those who thrive in this discipline have an incredible capacity to channel their goals with laser-like precision, transforming abstract ideas into practical accomplishments. They establish a strong link between their conscious mind and the subconscious source of creativity by maintaining persistent attention and emotional commitment.

The Alchemist's Forge: Core Principles of Creative Power

The human mind functions like an alchemy lab, transforming basic impulses into breakthrough ideas. Here are the essential concepts that drive this transformational process:

The Guiding Star: The Duality of Purpose

At the core of every great creative effort lies a master purpose—a guiding star whereby one lights his way. In this manner, the goal flares as a double flame: once sparking synthetic imagination—the world of trial and error—and another time, creative imagination, that little spark of creativity. Imagine a lighthouse with two kinds of beams: one straight and continuous, showing the relentless pursuit of a certain goal, and the other, a blinding flash that cuts through the darkness and symbolizes the sudden, unexpected born-from-imagination discovery. Fanned by passion's flames, these two forces combine to drive the intellect toward creation and discovery.

The Sculptor's Resolve: The Power of Persistence

Much like the sculptor chipping away at that block of stone, persistence is laid at the very bedrock of creative imagination. It is the unstoppable force turning raw concepts into stunning breakthroughs. The best inventors have this incredible ability to focus on one idea and overcome difficulties with sheer will. Their perseverance can act as a key to unlock doors to life-changing ideas. It is like a sculptor chiseling away; each act of perseverance brings him closer to realizing that piece, the masterpiece.

The Spark of Empathy: Fanning the Flames of Creativity

When sympathy is linked to some burning cause, it becomes a great stimulant of creative genius. Consider a burning fire, rich in latent potentiality. A gentle breeze infused with compassion and sympathy reignites the flame, transforming it into a blazing power of innovation. Many of history's most significant discoveries and triumphs over adversity were driven by causes much greater than personal gain, sometimes even to obsessive levels. Deep empathy fueled this relentless pursuit, the kind that inspired artistic ingenuity in the face of surmountable hurdles.

The Unrelenting Desire: Motive as the Master Key

An obsession fueled by a definitive motive is the key to unlocking the full potential of creative desire. Consider a complicated lock that only the correct key—forged with unshakeable purpose—can unlock. This burning desire is not a passing whim but a profoundly ingrained energy that pulls the individual onwards. Every great accomplishment begins with a clear motivation—the germ from which desire blooms. Consider Elon Musk's pursuits in space exploration and renewable energy. His robust and unwavering purpose—creating life multi-planetary and battling climate change—drives his unrelenting innovation via companies like SpaceX and Tesla.

The Whispering Subconscious: A Tireless Ally

The subconscious mind works tirelessly to render such a service to the burning desire, acting like a detective who never gives up and searches through all available resources to find the needed information. It doesn't make miracles from scratch already, but being immensely resourceful, it uses all possible ways to achieve what is desired. Imagine a massive library with shelves loaded with forgotten wisdom. Driven by an intense need for solutions, the subconscious mind relentlessly explores these shelves for the insights required to generate revolutionary ideas.

Continuing the Exploration of the Alchemist's Forge...

Our journey to the center of creative imagination continues. Now, we'll explore the concepts that allow individuals to turn raw thoughts into reality.

The Alchemist's Riddle: The Law of Equivalent Exchange

Each challenge and obstacle inherently possesses the potential for corresponding benefits. This concept harkens back to the ancient insights of alchemists: to manifest something of true value, one must be willing to relinquish something of comparable significance. Envision a treasure chest hidden within the intricate pathways of a labyrinth; the greater the peril encountered on the journey, the more substantial the reward awaiting at the end. Comparably, the most significant and transformative innovations often emerge from the challenges and adversities faced. Our challenges inspire us to engage in creative thinking, access hidden reservoirs of ingenuity, and ultimately undergo personal and societal evolution.

The Harmony of Minds: The Symphony of Collective Intelligence

Intellectual synergy acts similarly to an orchestra, with each instrument contributing its voice to produce a harmonic symphony. Similarly, when people with different viewpoints work together, they strengthen the collective problem-solving process. This collaboration enables people to build on one another's skills, stimulating creativity and quickening development. Imagine a team of scientists, each an expert in their discipline, collaborating to solve the universe's secrets. Their combined intelligence creates a synergy considerably stronger than its separate components, propelling discoveries to new heights.

The Uncommon Spark: The Rarity of Creative Imagination

Creative imagination is a rare and valuable talent in a world filled with the familiar. Those who can use this potential to produce new ideas—or revitalize old ones—hold the key to determining their future. Developing the creative imagination is an investment in personal fulfillment and financial independence. While copying previous thoughts is ubiquitous, the capacity to generate new ideas distinguishes individuals, laying the route for a life marked by creativity and achievement.

The Seed of Action: Personal Initiative

On the back of every great idea is the personal initiative driving it. It transforms fleeting thoughts into tangibles—what gets something from concept into creation. It's the drive that keeps treading on ideas until they come into being. Take, for example, a scientist who has developed some radical theory. Unless he has the initiative to test the theory, collect data, and present the results, the theory is just an intellectual plaything. Personal initiative is the backbone of creativity—the force moving ideas from the realm of imagination into the world of action.

From Spark to Flame: The Manifestation of Ideas

Transforming concepts into tangible outcomes requires a blend of imaginative thinking, focused effort, and careful planning. Yet, the genesis of most groundbreaking concepts often lies within the solitary flicker of creativity ignited in an individual's mind. Imagine an artist meticulously chiseling away at a raw block of stone, revealing a breathtaking masterpiece within. Though skill and method hold significance, it is the initial vision—the mental image within the sculptor's mind—that ignites the creative process.

Unveiling the Alchemist's Tools: Applications of Creative Imagination

The human mind's creative forge can be ignited for a multitude of purposes. Here, we explore some of the most common applications of creative imagination and the psychological forces that fuel them:

The Alchemical Compass: Definiteness of Purpose and Financial Dreams

A crystal-clear purpose acts like a compass and orients the imagination toward the set goals. Where the desire for financial independence lights the creative furnace, the mind becomes a powerful forge from which ideas could be hammered into wealth-creating tools. Imagine the expert alchemist laboring painstakingly to turn base metals into gold. Similarly, that focused desire lights the creative furnace, and one's imagination comes up with innovative solutions leading to the avenue of financial success.

The Synergy Symphony: Harmonizing Thoughts for Breakthroughs

It's the intellectual synergy principle or, in a looser sense, the "round table." Ideas flow into, intertwine with, and get woven into each other just like in an orchestra with collaboration among musicians that produces a richer sound. Myriad minds come together and strike out what's impossible with single contributors. Idea exchange in an intellectual crucible acts as a harmonizing force—a hammering place for solutions to the hardest challenges. For example, think of a group of scientists from different subjects to work out a highly demanding problem statement. The synergy brought about by the views of each one of these diversified disciplines released new avenues to problem-solving.

The Relentless Pursuit: Striving for Excellence or Perfection

The pursuit of perfection serves as a powerful catalyst for the creative mind. When individuals persist in their quest for accomplishment, the drive to surpass oneself naturally fosters the emergence of fresh thoughts and innovative ideas. This relentless pursuit of excellence drives creativity to its limits, ultimately fostering growth and evolution. Envision an artist, devoted and meticulous, gradually revealing the beauty hidden within a raw block of stone, crafting a masterpiece that others will recognize and admire. His pursuit of excellence will propel him toward innovative techniques and fresh perspectives in his craft.

The Spark of Belief: Faith as Fuel for Innovation

Embracing belief - that's the catalyst that ignites the flames of creativity. Without nourishment for belief, the imaginative essence remains dormant, leaving the inner flame devoid of warmth and vitality. The essence of belief activates the creative process, transforming that belief into the desired outcome, manifesting in the universe. Envision a researcher standing at the threshold of a groundbreaking revelation. They hold a firm conviction in their theory, inspiring and driving themselves to unleash their creative instincts to conquer every challenge that comes their way.

The Blueprint of Imagination: Self-Awareness and Organized Action

Organizational behavior is largely based on the power of the creative imagination. Direction from the self, through the use of imagination, ensures the effectiveness of planning and implementation. Imagine an architect making a blueprint with great elaboration. The finished structure has to be visualized by the architect to give shape to the project. Similarly, in any organization, that is the process toward success—the putting-vision-into-action process, powered by creative imagination and self-awareness.

Unveiling the Spark: Sources of Imagination Ignition

The human mind is a vast, fertile land yet to be cultivated. But where do the seeds of creativity first take root? Here, we explore some of the most potent forces that ignite the spark of the imagination.

The Double-Edged Sword: Fear

Fear serves as a potent double-edged sword in the landscape of our imagination. It can strike us like a jolt, flooding our system with adrenaline and propelling us into extraordinary acts of creativity when our existence hangs in the balance. Envision a climber teetering on the brink of an unfathomable chasm: the survival instinct ignites a surge of creativity, conjuring visions of escape and ingenious solutions previously unimagined. At times, fear can lead to a completely different outcome. The paralyzing grip of fear halts the mind, ensnaring the imagination in a chilling embrace of anxiety. The imagination often finds itself immobilized, much like a deer frozen in the glare of headlights, leaving us struggling to access our most insightful responses to the challenge at hand.

The Phoenix Rising: Failure and Resilience

Sometimes, the sting of failure can be the most potent catalyst for the imagination. Setbacks sometimes act as fiery forges for rethinking, adaptation, and innovation. Consider the phoenix, that mythical creature reborn from the ashes, more powerful. It can set fire to a burning desire to overcome, to steer among the shifting sands, and to let loose creative potential. Still, it will not always be. Furthermore, this also creates distrust, disbelief, and discouragement, causing the dampening of creativity and hindering us from moving on further upon repeated failures.

The Clever Asking: Ingenious Techniques and Thoughtful Inquiries

Individuals endowed with the capacity for creative imagination adeptly employ guiding questions that illuminate their imaginative faculties, enabling them to address challenges or forge pathways toward innovative concepts. Engaging the mind in a context that transcends mere contemplation of the superficial aspects of an endeavor, these inquiries illustrate compelling scenarios that illuminate the advantages and strategies for achieving desired outcomes.

Proficient sales professionals understand the art of employing guiding questions that ignite the imaginative faculties of potential customers. Engaging customers in a manner that transcends mere product consideration, these inquiries craft vivid scenarios that effectively illuminate the product's advantages. Envision a sales professional showcasing the features of an innovative automobile. The salesperson might encourage the customer to envision a thrilling ride along the highway, experiencing the exhilaration of the wind in their hair while enjoying unparalleled comfort and performance. Strategic inquiry effectively steers consumer cognition, fostering a desire for the product while igniting the customer's imagination.

The Unquenchable Thirst: Curiosity and the Unknown

The innate human drive for curiosity stands as one of our most fundamental needs, serving as a potent catalyst for the flourishing of imagination. The profound enigmas of the universe, largely uncharted by humanity, have captivated numerous religious traditions, scientific endeavors, and artistic explorations. This drive compels us to delve deeper and expand the horizons of human understanding. Consider, for instance, the young individual who looks skyward at the vast expanse of stars and is profoundly affected by the enormity of the cosmos. Nonetheless, it fosters a profound curiosity within individuals to explore the universe, initiating a process of imagination that ignites a continuous desire for knowledge throughout their lives.

The Mirror Within: Self-Expression and Empathy

Self-expression, whether in writing, orally, or other arts, has become one constant stimulant of imagination. Ordering our thoughts into communicative form, whether verbal or non-verbal, fosters creativity even in childhood. Think of a child drawing with crayons. Shapes and colors form to represent emotions and experiences. This playful act of expression of their surroundings helps to cultivate imagination so they interpret and deal with the world around them. But over time, this process grows, deepened by empathy—a step into someone else's perspective. The ability to walk in somebody's shoes and mirror the thoughts and feelings of others expands imaginative horizons. A writer shapes a fictional character in much the same way that we do—seeing with the eyes of another—through the act of inhabiting his world. Combining self-expression and empathy can release all of one's potential creatively and further deepen one's understanding of oneself and the human experience.[6]

The Primal Urge: Adversity and Hunger

The experiences of hunger and hardship serve as fundamental aspects that ignite the imagination across all life forms. The phenomenon of hunger serves as a remarkably effective catalyst, rooted in its status as a fundamental drive. In moments of scarcity, it is fascinating to observe how the human imagination engages in a remarkable process of creativity, strategizing ways to procure nourishment and ensure survival. Imagine a solitary hiker navigating the dense wilderness, surrounded by towering trees and the sounds of nature. Their imaginations infer that this region likely possesses elements of significant value for consumption. They proceed to devise a strategy for locating sustenance while concurrently formulating a plan to ensure their safe return home. In the intricate tapestry of survival, instinct and imagination emerge as coexisting forces that play a pivotal role across all species.[7]

---

[6] The role of self-expression and mirroring in supporting children's imagination development is crucial. These faculties not only allow children to express their creativity but also provide a platform for them to learn and grow through mirroring others.

[7] Imagination Across Life Forms. From the tiniest microorganisms to complex organisms, imagination, and instinct intertwine, ensuring survival and adaptation.

The Sharpened Lens: Focus and Imagination

A sharp focus can awaken the imagination like a laser beam cutting through mental fog. When our focus is glued to one problem or object, our imagination gets into the act—searching for solutions and coming up with new perspectives. Think of a scientist working on a microscope who is concentrating on some biological specimen. He lights the match of his focused attention on that, which may result in a discovery of groundbreaking potential.

Think of Thomas Edison, who kept trying until he found the light bulb after hundreds of hours of focused experimentation. The concentration of his attention on a singular problem turned his imagination into an invention. Or take an artist who carefully looks at some landscape and eventually, by concentrated effort, carries out the scene on a canvas with vivid colors. In each instance, focused attention allows the imagination to tap deeper into deeper insights and, hence, harness its fuller power in creation.

Building Bridges of Imagination: Hypotheses and Unassailable Truths

The essence of scientific exploration lies in hypothetical thinking, which involves the ability to ponder "what if" scenarios. By formulating interpretations for the phenomena we observe, we create a connection between our current understanding and the mysteries that still elude us. These instances, presently speculative notions, chart a course toward unveiling irrefutable reality. Imagine a keen observer thoughtfully dissecting the intricacies of the situation at hand. People tap into their creative abilities to develop different theories about what happened, ultimately piecing together the truth to clarify the mystery. Individuals with deep expertise in diverse fields—including legal professionals, jurists, researchers, and medical practitioners—are called to participate in this imaginative endeavor to foster breakthroughs and reach conclusive insights.

Exploring the Intrinsic Potential: The Universal Nature of Imagination

The human mind encompasses a vast and enigmatic domain: Imagination. Like a sculptor's chisel, this remarkable faculty shapes our worldview and intricately carves out our creative potential. It is indeed a fascinating observation that certain individuals seem to possess an inexhaustible reservoir of creative imagination. This leads us to the critical inquiry of whether such imaginative capacity is innate or if it is cultivated and enhanced through environmental influences and experiences.

It is encouraging to note that, akin to other cognitive abilities, imagination functions as a muscle that strengthens through consistent practice. Neglecting to utilize this essential tool can significantly diminish its effectiveness. Just as a sculptor who ceases to engage with his craft may experience a decline in his skills, an imagination that remains dormant will inevitably become less agile.

The advantages of a vibrant imagination extend well beyond simple whimsy. Robust imaginative faculties endow individuals with a remarkably potent form of "opportunity radar." By honing their ability to envision possibilities, individuals cultivate a skill set that enables them to identify circumstances aligned with their objectives and ambitions. This heightened sensitivity represents merely the initial phase of a broader process. An imaginative mindset serves as a catalyst for initiative, driving the pursuit of opportunities and transforming them into tangible outcomes through deliberate action.

THE UNSEEN ARCHITECT: UNVEILING THE INNER WORLD OF THE CREATIVE MIND

ఠఠఠ

Unveiling the Alchemist's Vision: Ideas and Impact

S uch is the power and the possibility in this thing called creative vision. Let us delve deeper into the essence and the deep impact.

The Magnetic Muse: Creative Vision and the Law of Attraction

Creative vision acts as a magnet, drawing unto it all we want and desire. It is at the heart of the Law of Attraction. When we consciously work on developing a clear creative vision, we become a point of attraction—a beacon calling toward us the very resources and opportunities we need to manifest our dreams. Picture the sculptor who envisions in his mind's eye what his sculpture will look like. His inner vision then serves as a magnet that attracts the tools, materials, and inspiration he requires to bring his creation forth into his life.

The Wand of Wonder: Unlocking the Miracle Within

Creative vision rests quietly within us, like a wand of miracles, concealed in the mind's hidden sanctuary. It stands ready for the moment of awakening, the catalyst that unleashes our intrinsic brilliance. Upon activation, this vision serves as a pathway to remarkable accomplishments. Envision the minds of those who stand at the precipice of revolutionary insights. As individuals expand their creative vision, it transforms into a powerful tool, unlocking the concealed mysteries of existence and guiding them toward innovation.

The Inner Genie: Awakening the Creative Spark

Within each individual lies a metaphorical Aladdin's lamp, acting as a source of unexploited creative potential. By recognizing this inherent power, we activate the creative energies that encourage us to reflect inwardly and begin the path of personal exploration. A creative vision beckons the aware, urging us to embark on meaningful exploration and immerse ourselves in the depths of our imagination. Imagine a scenario where a creative writer encounters a moment of stagnation. Delving into the depths of one's creative vision and contemplating the most significant questions can act as a powerful spark for uncovering fresh sources of inspiration and rekindling a passion for storytelling.

The Keen Eye: Recognizing and Seizing Opportunities

Through a lens of imaginative insight, we can uncover opportunities that resonate with our aspirations for goal-setting. It sharpens awareness, allowing an individual to identify a possible pathway to achievement. The ability to identify opportunities is merely one facet of the broader vision. Rather, imaginative insight fosters the courage and resolve essential for seizing these opportunities, combined with an innocent enthusiasm to transform them into reality. Reflect on an entrepreneur with a clear and compelling vision for his enterprise. Their creative perspective enables them to identify emerging market trends and develop strategies to leverage them, propelling their venture forward.

Shaping Destiny: From Thoughts to Habits

The creative vision is a power in itself, transcending the plane of ideas. It refines our thoughts into plans. Those plans become the building blocks of habits, relentless actions driving us toward goal accomplishment. After a while, those habits become the weavings in the fabric of our destiny. Think about an athlete who pictures himself or herself winning the Olympics. Their creative vision—a habit—translates into a rigorous regime of training, which leads to the peak of performance and potential achievement of their dreams.

Soaring Beyond Boundaries: The Power of Imagination to Transcend Limitations

The Wright brothers did not enter the world with wings, yet they possessed a far more formidable asset—Creative Vision, enabling them to transcend conventional limitations. This innovative spirit, functioning as a catalyst, played a crucial role in overcoming the potential constraints of the human body, enabling us to rise resiliently against the pull of gravity. Wings of flesh were unnecessary, for they had, much earlier, conceived a notion of flight within their minds—a cognitive framework that would nurture ceaseless innovation. Much like the imaginative minds that created the first airplane, we now witness how creative vision can transcend seemingly insurmountable challenges. The Wright brothers exemplify the notion that it is not merely the presence of constraints that defines our journey but rather our capacity to imagine possibilities that lie beyond those constraints that drive progress.

Muscles Follow Mind: The Power of Brainpower

While physical strength holds significance, the intellectual prowess fueled by an innovative vision serves as the genuine catalyst for advancement. While muscle power holds significance on its own, it represents merely one of the instruments directed by the intellect that determines its effective utilization. Consider a skilled athlete: mere physical strength does not guarantee triumph; his strategic insight and creative foresight enable him to outsmart competitors and achieve victory. The mind-muscle connection underscores a fundamental principle: while strength propels us onward, it is the creative vision of our minds that ultimately determines our trajectory. In a rapidly evolving world where innovation is paramount, the role of imagination has become crucial in driving progress and addressing the challenges that confront us.

Sharpening the Alchemist's Eye: Factors for Enhanced Creative Vision[8]

The single greatest source of creative vision, the basis of personal success, thrives only amid certain circumstances. Let us learn about them a little and observe how they create a more vibrant creative energy:

The Keen Eye: Recognizing Opportunities

An alert mind serves as the foundational pathway to creative vision, characterized by discernment and the pursuit of opportunities. This signifies a transformation in our perspective—an elevation of our awareness regarding the surrounding world—thereby empowering

---

[8] Innovative Insight is not a static trait but a dynamic process that can be cultivated and refined. It requires a blend of introspection, collaboration, and action. By integrating these principles, one can sharpen their innovative insight, turning it into a powerful tool for personal and professional growth.

us to discern those subtle avenues leading to success. This image captures an entrepreneur who is perpetually vigilant for emerging market trends. Individuals consistently proactively search for potential disruptions, aiming to devise innovative solutions that can yield a competitive advantage through a visionary approach.

The Focused Embrace: Purpose and Action

The essence of creative vision is indeed remarkable; however, it is significantly enhanced when anchored in a clear and defined purpose. When we clearly understand our goals, our cognitive processes sharpen, enabling us to readily recognize opportunities that align with our ambitions. The clarity in our vision elevates it from a mere passive aspiration to a vibrant and dynamic catalyst, steering us toward a clearly defined destination. Consider, for example, this researcher dedicated to discovering a cure for a particular disease. It not only maintains the effort but also enhances one's perception.

With a well-defined purpose guiding their thoughts, they possess the ability to identify promising research avenues that may escape the notice of others, recognize potential breakthroughs in emerging studies, or draw connections between seemingly unrelated data—insights that might otherwise go unnoticed. This clarity of purpose serves as a cognitive filter, enabling individuals to evaluate opportunities based on their potential value versus the risk of distraction. In this manner, purpose functions as a lens through which individuals perceive the world, granting insight into future pathways that might have otherwise remained obscured.

The Strategic Mind: Planning and Action

Creative vision isn't simply about inspiration; it also demands methodical planning. Each step should be part of a deliberate strategy, ensuring that our actions are not random but contribute to a larger purpose. Imagine an artist embarking on a new project.

Their creative vision guides them, but they also create detailed sketches and plans, ensuring their artistic journey unfolds with focus and intention.

The Collective Spark: Synergy and Shared Knowledge

When fueled by intellectual synergy, collaboration becomes a potent force for creative vision. By tapping into the collective wisdom, experiences, and insights of others, we broaden our knowledge base and unlock fresh perspectives that we might not have discovered alone. Imagine a team of writers gathered to brainstorm ideas for a new story.

As they exchange thoughts and build on each other's suggestions, new creative pathways are sparked, allowing them to craft a richer and more compelling narrative than any of them could have created individually. This shared exchange of ideas doesn't just add more voices to the mix—it multiplies the creative potential, leading to breakthroughs that elevate the entire project.

The Unwavering Spirit: Faith and Openness

Applied faith ushers in creative vision, pushing us past the threshold of fear and mental limitation. The more faith we adopt, the more we open ourselves to being guided and inspired—by intuition, a deep reservoir of personal knowledge, or even a spiritual belief system. More concretely, it comes in the form of trust in the process, even when the impossible stares us in the face.

Consider an inventor faced with a technical barrier. Their belief in their ultimate vision keeps them open to radical ideas and solutions, allowing them to think outside the box. Instead of doubt paralyzing them, faith drives them to experiment anew until a breakthrough reaches fruition. The blend of faith and openness acts as a catalyst for innovation. Where others might give up, this interaction between faith and openness empowers creativity to blossom.

The Extra Mile Magnet: Exceeding Expectations

Extending our efforts opens pathways that enhance our imaginative perspective. We cultivate a reputation that generates momentum by consistently exceeding expectations, attracting even greater opportunities. Envision the individual in customer service who consistently transcends expectations to support clients. Their readiness to develop innovative, tailored solutions for clients fosters a deeper connection with customers and recognizes their role within the organization.

As time progresses, a reputation built on innovation and dedication will naturally lead to promotions and leadership opportunities while inspiring the pursuit of new initiatives. Exceeding expectations not only motivates those around us but also elevates the quality of service, positioning individuals as key players in the advancement and prosperity of the organization. The collective impact of these actions amplifies their influence, drawing in additional opportunities for development and creativity.

The Current Rhythm: Awareness and Expectation

The creative vision reveals a deep awareness of the present circumstances. It is intriguing to reflect on how we can truly imagine a brighter future by nurturing an awareness of our current realities while also deeply comprehending the needs and desires of our community. Envision a trailblazer in fashion, shaping trends and impacting styles. He does not simply follow current trends; instead, he thoughtfully analyzes their social and cultural implications to identify the styles likely to connect with consumers in the near future.

The Self-Starter: Internal Drive

The core drivers behind creative vision are the intrinsic desire to pursue one's passions and the proactive steps taken to bring those ideas to fruition. It is the inner drive that propels our efforts, rather than outside forces, that enables our creative potential to thrive genuinely. Imagine an artist immersed in sculpting, driven solely by the desire to express oneself, free from the need for outside approval. His inner drive inspires him to delve into new creative paths with exceptional insight.

The Responsible Alchemist: Ownership and Accountability

Taking full responsibility for one's actions is a cornerstone of creative vision. This ownership intuitively serves as the foundation for decision-making and motivates success in creative projects. Although that requires seeking other advice and utilizing the intellectual synergy principle in collaboration and multiple perspectives, personal responsibility for the direction and results of the project remains individual.

Imagine an entrepreneur embarking on a new venture; they might turn to mentors for guidance, collaborate with a team, or engage with stakeholders for insights. Ultimately, they are responsible for key decisions and the overarching direction of the business. This sense of responsibility permeates every facet of the endeavor, influencing everything from overarching strategies to the minutiae of daily operations. This approach guarantees that choices are made with a comprehensive understanding of potential risks and rewards, fostering a forward-thinking mentality that promotes continuous growth and enhancement. By embracing his own creative journey, an entrepreneur navigates challenges effectively and cultivates dedication and resilience, fostering a similar ethos within his team.

This profound sense of responsibility enables an individual to make informed decisions and adapt strategies as needed, guiding the project toward success. It is essential to manifest creative vision by ensuring every decision aligns with the task at hand. It nurtures creativity, propels progress, and ultimately reveals the obstacles faced and the insights gained along the journey.

The Duality of Imagination: Synthesis and Creation

The interplay of duality within the realm of imagination significantly enhances one's creative vision. On the one hand, a synthetic faculty allows individuals to deconstruct existing concepts and reconstruct them innovatively. Conversely, the creative capacity empowers us to generate entirely novel concepts. The potential for creativity expands significantly when we harness both dimensions of our imaginative capabilities. Consider the scenario of a composer engaged in the process of crafting an original composition.

In conclusion, creative vision is a complex and multifaceted phenomenon. By cultivating a growth mindset, embracing collaboration, and fostering a spirit of self-motivation and responsibility, we can nurture this powerful force and embark on a lifelong journey of learning, innovation, and achievement.

The Alchemist's Journey: Time Scale and Process for a Creative Vision

The blossoming of a potent creative vision within a civilization is a slow process, not a particular spark. Now, let's look at the possible timeline and the challenges:

Cultivating Creative Vision: A Philosophical Journey for Patience

Developing a strong creative vision is akin to the careful artistry of a skilled vinegar master. It requires dedication to patience and meticulous cultivation over an extended period. Imagine a society steadily developing a philosophical foundation rooted in the ideals of creativity and innovation. The realization of this philosophy will not occur overnight; instead, it will evolve through a sustained process of refinement and development fueled by meticulous research, experimentation, and meaningful discourse over the years. The evolution of this philosophical foundation, akin to the intricate aging process of a fine Balsamic Vinegar, necessitates a considerable duration to attain its fullest depth and richness.

The Silent Seed: The Period of Indifference

After the initial surge of creativity, one might experience a period marked by apathy. Just as the light from distant stars takes time to journey through the immense expanse of space before it reaches our vision, so too does the impact of a new way of thinking, which often requires a moment of contemplation before it is completely acknowledged and appreciated. Yet, this state of "indifference" could provide fertile ground for growth. Imagine a community immersed in vibrant dialogue, grappling with groundbreaking ideas that challenge traditional boundaries. One might experience initial pushback or a lack of understanding. In this seemingly serene period, the foundation for profound transformation is laid, preparing for forthcoming progress.

The Catalyst of Change: Awakening from Crisis

A significant crisis frequently catalyzes societal awakening, revealing the transformative potential of innovative, creative visions. During periods of disruption and unpredictability, individuals tend to exhibit a greater openness to innovative concepts and unconventional methodologies. Envision a community grappling with the aftermath of a natural disaster, facing significant challenges in its recovery efforts. A previously neglected philosophy that prioritizes vitality and creativity may suddenly discover a crucial role, signaling a pathway toward renewal and advancement. Catastrophe serves as a catalyst for individuals to reassess their values and embrace innovative perspectives.

The emergence of a powerful creative vision within a society unfolds as a gradual and sustained journey. It demands a deep sense of patience, unwavering perseverance, and an openness to change's transformative nature. By nurturing an environment of questioning, teamwork, and receptivity, a community can create the essential conditions for innovative ideas to thrive, steering them toward a more promising tomorrow.

The Creative Spirit in Faith: Bridging Tradition and Discovery

The human spirit seems to yearn for the comfort of tradition and the excitement of unknown discovery. More than perhaps anywhere else, this innate duality finds extremely sharp expression within precincts of faith, where mysteries of existence converge with psychological underpinnings of belief. Let us trace out a tapestry of creative vision interwoven into the fabric of religious experience.

Whispers in the Sanctuary: Reimagining Rituals

An uneasy feeling resonates through the hallowed halls of religious institutions as whispers of doubt and the urge for deeper meaning echo within ancient rituals. It is a creative vision calling them to re-examine practices that had become rote and opaque. This supplies the opportunity to unlock anew the psychological power of faith.

- **Cracking the Code of Ritual:** Often, religious practices degenerate into ritualistic behavior bereft of their meaning and import. Artistic expression insists that we take a closer look at the psychology behind these rituals. By rediscovering their symbolic meaning and emotional resonance, we can retrieve our sense of awe and wonder. Consider a religious ceremony transformed into an immersive performance that elicits an emotional response and creates a shared experience.

- **Beyond the Veil: Revealing the Enigma.** Numerous spiritual paths are enveloped in an enigma adorned with teachings and rituals cloaked in symbolic significance. Great creative vision encourages us to engage with these mysteries not as strict doctrines but as opportunities for psychological exploration. By fostering open dialogue, promoting critical thinking, and allowing for personal interpretation, religious institutions can enable individuals to create their own significant connections with the divine.

The Shepherd and the Seeker: A Psychological Dance

The dynamic between spiritual guides and their adherents unfolds as a multifaceted psychological interplay. Innovative insight can enable spiritual leaders to transform from mere guides of their community into catalysts for personal development.

- **Transitioning from Pulpit to Psyche:** The conventional sermon structure, laden with declarations and assertions, frequently appears disconnected and lacks relevance. The innovative perspective compels spiritual leaders to formulate communications that resonate with the internal psychological struggles faced by their communities. In addressing contemporary concerns, offering strategies to navigate life's challenges, and facilitating a space for dialogue, clergy can assume the role of a reliable confidant and guide.

- **The Masks of Faith:** Individuals frequently adopt the façades of piety within religious spaces, driven by the apprehension of judgment or the potential for alienation. The cultivation of creative vision plays a pivotal role in creating an environment conducive to psychological vulnerability. Engaging in open discussions surrounding doubt, struggles with faith, and the intricate nature of belief allows religious institutions to cultivate a more genuine community that offers meaningful support.

A Sacred Rebellion: Redefining the Narrative

The essence of humanity is inherently defiant, constantly seeking to challenge and reshape the established norms. The intrinsic wiring of an individual can transform into a profound act of defiance within the realm of belief.

- **Breaking through the stained-glass ceiling,** we observe that traditional religious narratives frequently polarize and rarely encapsulate their communities' diverse experiences and perspectives. The infusion of creative vision facilitates reimagining narratives, incorporating diverse perspectives highlighting pressing contemporary social issues. Embracing the perspectives of marginalized communities and fostering inclusive leadership represents a significant avenue through which religious institutions can revitalize their meaning and cultivate deeper connections with individuals. This approach enhances the relevance of faith and ensures a psychologically safe environment for everyone involved.

- **The Unmasking of Fear:** Fears, frequently cloaked in religious contexts, may drive compliance; however, they often serve as barriers to spiritual development. Engaging with creative vision compels individuals to confront their fears head-on. To put it differently, it is beneficial for religious institutions to encourage critical thinking and facilitate an open exchange of ideas regarding the psychological roots of fear. This approach can lead to the development of more meaningful and authentic relationships between congregations and their faiths. This transition enables the movement from a compliance rooted in fear to a personally enriching and deeply comprehended faith.

In conclusion, by embracing creative vision and a commitment to serving the needs of their communities, religious institutions can illuminate a vibrant and relevant path for people of faith in the 21st century.

Illuminating the Path: A Psychological Tapestry of Faith

Recognizing the pursuit of enlightenment in religious practices highlights the significance of exploring the psychological aspects of this transformation. Here's how imaginative insight can illuminate a more purposeful journey:

From Existential Dread to Existential Hope: A Psychological Shift

Religious institutions have often focused on the fear of death and the afterlife, creating a sense of existential dread for many. Creative vision compels a turning to the inculcation of existential hope. By touting the beauty and wonder of life, providing support systems to navigate life's challenges, and offering a sense of purpose, religious institutions can empower people to live life more meaningfully.

- **Dealing with the Vanished:** Ultimately, evading the reality of death does not eliminate its presence. Innovative perspectives foster more mentally sound approaches to address the challenges we face. Engaging in open conversations about mortality and the process of grief counseling allows individuals to face their fears and discover a sense of comfort. Spiritual communities often provide gatherings and practices for those in mourning, fostering a sense of resolution and understanding.

Beyond Words: The Power of Action in a Suffering World

Numerous religious doctrines often remain at the level of rhetoric, revealing their limitations when confronted with the harsh realities of suffering in the world. The manifestation of creative vision underscores the imperative to take action. Translating faith into service activities enables religious institutions to manifest a profound sense of purpose alongside the psychological advantages of aiding others.

- **Healing Through Deeds:** Engaging in meaningful actions, such as organized volunteering initiatives, social justice efforts, and interfaith collaborations, provides compelling examples of how individuals can address pressing real-world issues like poverty and illness. These experiences foster community connections and facilitate a deeper engagement with one's faith. Such acts of service provide relief and cultivate a sense of community and shared purpose among individuals.

The Synergy of Wisdom: A Council of Collaboration

Quite often, religious institutions result in silos, thereby reducing their overall potential impact. The creative vision envisages the constitution of an "intellectual synergy group." This would consist of various professionals, such as doctors, lawyers, business leaders, etc., who could provide a holistic view of community needs and propose practical solutions.

- **Breaking Down Walls:** The religious community can facilitate collaboration between the leadership of faith-based organizations and communities, social workers, and psychologists to create a more psychologically informed approach toward solving important social issues. Collaboration can also help to bridge social divides and engender a sense of unity within the community.

From Sermons to Symphonies: Reimagining Religious Discourse

The traditional sermon format seems remote and irrelevant. Creative vision challenges religious leaders to create a message relevant to their people's psychological realities.

- **The Symphony of Service:** Religious leaders can transform sermons into passionate advocacy that bridges the connection between faith and its application in practice. They could further enhance this religious experience with storytelling, activities, and current issues, making it more vibrant and relevant.

In summary, by embracing an unwavering acceptance of creative vision alongside a focus on practical action, psychological wellness, and a comprehensive approach to community challenges, religious organizations can provide essential guidance to individuals of faith navigating the complexities of the 21st century.

THE ARCHITECTS OF INNOVATION: TRAITS OF THE VISIONARY MIND

 δ❧δ❧δ❧

C reative visionaries are the forerunners of a better future. They possess exceptional qualities that propel them beyond the ordinary, transforming ideas into groundbreaking realities. As we delve into the hallmarks of these extraordinary individuals, we'll explore how they shape our future, uncover the mysteries behind civilizational progress, and initiate creative visions that turn reflection into impactful action.

Beyond the Ordinary: Hallmarks of Creative Visionaries Shaping Our Future

People with visionary qualities will shape our future; they are able to see beyond the obvious. These remarkable people have the power to show the way forward, endure the worst storms, and bring harmony out of turmoil. They motivate people to achieve new heights by being insatiably curious, optimistic, and fearlessly ambitious.

Organized into key categories, we will explore the hallmarks of these creative visionaries: The Visionary Mindset, where we uncover the intrinsic traits that empower visionaries to think beyond limits and redefine the possible; Inspiring and Empowering

Others, discovering how visionaries ignite the potential within others and guide them toward greatness; Innovative Action and Transformation, witnessing the extraordinary ways visionaries turn ideas into reality and navigate the complexities of progress; Creating Impact and Legacy, learning how visionaries leave an indelible mark on the world, shaping societies and cultures for generations to come; Visionary Leadership and Collaboration, exploring the collaborative spirit that allows visionaries to build bridges, unite communities, and drive collective progress; and Personal and Societal Growth, delving into the personal journeys of visionaries as they foster growth, balance, and innovation in both themselves and society.

First Category: The Visionary Mindset

1. Treasure Trove of Ideas: The Currency of Innovation

Innovators perceive concepts as the driving force behind advancement. Just as a discerning investor recognizes the potential in promising ventures, a forward-thinking individual perceives strong ideas as the foundational elements of innovation. These concepts emerge from a fusion of curiosity and unwavering inquiry, subsequently honed through trial and collective engagement.

Consider the dynamic between Steve Jobs and Steve Wozniak, for example. Their perspective on the personal computer transformed technology, democratizing access to computers for the everyday individual and indelibly altering the fabric of the tech industry. Their inquisitive nature regarding electronics and computing catalyzed the development of the Apple I, while their openness to experimentation and collaboration transformed that nascent concept into a groundbreaking innovation.

Another compelling illustration is Elon Musk, whose aspirations span sustainable energy and exploring outer space. His endeavors with Tesla and SpaceX illustrate the profound impact that innovative thinking can have on advancing various domains. Musk's profound inquiry into sustainable energy has catalyzed the emergence of electric vehicles, which are now revolutionizing the automotive landscape. In the realm of exploration, his deep-seated intrigue with the cosmos has propelled advancements in space travel, exemplified by SpaceX's groundbreaking achievements like the development of reusable rockets and ambitious visions for colonizing Mars.

These examples demonstrate that those with profound insight grasp the true value of their ideas. They cultivate their thoughts, understanding their intrinsic worth and the potential they hold for evolution into transformative breakthroughs. Through nurturing their inquisitive nature and engaging in collaborative efforts, they transform theoretical ideas into concrete, impactful realities that can change the world.

Visionaries such as Jobs, Wozniak, and Musk illuminate the profound truth that the essence of innovation is rooted in our ideas. An idea emerges when it is embraced with fervor, honed through exploration, and manifested through collective effort.

2. The Unbreakable Spirit: Weathering the Storms

In the presence of overwhelming challenges, the visionary individual embarks on their journey with renewed determination. They confront challenges directly, embracing adversity with courage. True resilience for a visionary lies not in evading obstacles but skillfully maneuvering them with unwavering resolve and creativity. They recognize that the most intense challenges serve as profound examinations of their commitment and ingenuity, and they welcome these trials as chances for personal evolution.

Consider the case of Thomas Edison. Countless setbacks marked his journey before he brought the lightbulb to life; each misstep was a vital lesson, propelling him forward rather than holding him back. Edison's steadfast determination and unwavering faith in his vision embody a genuine innovator's indomitable essence. His renowned statement, "I have not failed." "I've just discovered 10,000 methods that are ineffective," reflects his unwavering determination.

In a parallel vein, Elon Musk encountered numerous challenges during SpaceX's early rocket launches. Every setback presented significant financial and technical hurdles, yet Musk's resolve remained steadfast. He persevered through every challenge, extracting valuable lessons from each setback, ultimately leading to SpaceX's remarkable achievements, including the groundbreaking launch and landing of reusable rockets. Musk's resilience in the face of challenges and his unwavering determination have significantly advanced the frontiers of space exploration and innovation.

Bill Gates exemplifies an unwavering resilience that inspires many. Upon introducing its inaugural version of Windows, Microsoft encountered a wave of scrutiny and technical hurdles. Nonetheless, Gates' unwavering dedication to his vision for personal computing propelled him to consistently refine and enhance the software. This resilience established the groundwork for Microsoft's supremacy in the software sector.

In a parallel vein, the visionaries behind Google, Larry Page, and Sergey Brin, faced doubt and a myriad of technical challenges upon the initial unveiling of their search engine. Their unwavering resolve to enhance and innovate in the face of adversity culminated in establishing a tech company that has profoundly shaped the global landscape.

These instances demonstrate how those with a clear vision harness challenges as a catalyst to deepen their commitment to their aspirations. Their resilient essence is driven by steadfast resolve and intention, enabling them to traverse obstacles and rise with greater strength. Through accepting life's challenges, those with a profound vision transform barriers into opportunities that propel them toward their aspirations.

3. Rewriting the Impossible: The Language of Possibility

For the visionary, the term 'impossible' transforms into an invitation for exploration and growth. In the lexicon of those who dare to dream, the term "impossible" transforms into "opportunity"—a notion that elevates them from mediocrity to greatness. Every challenge presents itself as a riddle waiting to be solved, a chance to transform what appears unachievable into reality. Their unwavering conviction in potential allows them to turn obstacles into opportunities, uncovering avenues where others perceive only limitations.

Reflect on Bill Gates's journey and Microsoft's inception. Gates recognized the transformative possibilities of personal computers during an era when skepticism prevailed about their integration into everyday life. His steadfast conviction in this vision propelled him to create software that transformed the tech landscape, manifesting what once appeared to be an unlikely aspiration into a pervasive truth.

Consider the case of Larry Page and Sergey Brin, the visionaries behind Google, who provide yet another compelling illustration. Their aspiration to systematically arrange the vast expanse of global information and render it universally accessible appeared remarkably bold in that era. Their groundbreaking algorithms and unwavering commitment to their vision have redefined our relationship with information, turning the unattainable into reality.

Visionaries such as Steve Jobs, Elon Musk, Bill Gates, Larry Page, and Sergey Brin illuminate the path to understanding that what appears unattainable is simply an opportunity poised for exploration. Their capacity to transcend limitations and reinterpret obstacles as avenues for growth empowers them to create and accomplish remarkable achievements. By adopting a mindset centered on potential, those who envision the future consistently challenge the limits of achievement, encouraging each of us to reconsider our constraints.

4. Fearless Hearts: Embracing Challenges with Bravery

Their bravery resembles an expansive ocean, limitless and profound. Those who envision the future possess a courageous spirit. They confront challenges not with fear but with courage and confidence. It becomes evident that, in many instances, fear erects more obstacles to advancement than any other element. They remain steadfast, allowing nothing to sway their decisions or judgments. By embodying courage and taking decisive action, they inspire those around them to venture beyond familiar boundaries and confidently embrace challenges.

Reflect on Rosa Parks, whose courageous spirit ignited a transformative chapter in the struggle for civil rights. In a profound act of defiance, she remained seated on a segregated bus, confronting arrest with remarkable bravery. Her audacity confronted racial injustice and motivated countless individuals to pursue equality. Parks' courageous decision illustrated how a single act of fearlessness can ignite significant societal transformation.

In parallel, Larry Page and Sergey Brin, the visionaries behind Google, confronted obstacles with courage as they introduced their search engine into a fiercely competitive technological arena. In the face of doubt and intense rivalry, they embraced their aspirations with courage and creativity. Their audacious strategy reshaped Google into a technological powerhouse, fundamentally altering our relationship with information access.

Consider the case of Malala Yousafzai, who courageously challenged the Taliban's prohibition on girls' education in Pakistan. In the face of difficult circumstances, she remained steadfast in her commitment to championing education and women's rights. Malala's courageous spirit and steadfast dedication to her mission have motivated countless individuals across the globe and led to her receiving the Nobel Peace Prize.

These instances demonstrate how courageous people confront obstacles and motivate others to adopt courage. By choosing to rise above fear, they dismantle obstacles and create pathways for advancement. Their bravery initiates a profound influence, inspiring others to overcome obstacles with assurance and resolve.

5. Igniters of Willpower: Sparking Personal Initiative

Visionaries ignite the fire of resolve. They eliminate the core of defeatism by igniting the flame of personal initiative. The insightful individual motivates others, sparking a hunger to chase their dreams with steadfast resolve. There exists a profound belief in the innate possibilities within each person, inspiring others to take charge of their journeys.

Reflect on Mahatma Gandhi's profound impact. His steadfast dedication to nonviolent resistance ignited a movement that inspired countless individuals in India to pursue their quest for independence. Gandhi's conviction in the significance of personal agency and shared determination reshaped a nation, demonstrating the profound impact that visionary thinkers can have in inspiring widespread individual initiative.

Consider Richard Branson, the visionary behind the Virgin Group. Branson's entrepreneurial journey exemplifies a bold exploration of varied pursuits, ranging from the realms of music to the frontiers of space travel. His enthusiasm and self-assurance in his vision motivate others to embrace daring opportunities and pursue their true passions. Branson's conviction in the inherent potential of every individual to attain greatness cultivates an environment rich in innovation and proactive engagement.

Reflect on Malala Yousafzai's narrative in the landscape of education. Her unwavering commitment to promoting girls' education amidst significant challenges has sparked a worldwide movement. Malala's bold stance and steadfast conviction in the transformative potential of education inspire youth across the globe to advocate for their right to learn and to chase their aspirations.

These instances illustrate how those with a profound sense of purpose dispel feelings of hopelessness through their deeds and beliefs and ignite a sense of resolve in those around them. By cultivating a mindset that encourages personal initiative and the empowerment of individuals to steer their paths, those with a visionary outlook propel collective advancement and ignite profound transformation.

Second Category: Inspiring and Empowering Others

1. Lighthouses of Hope: Illuminating the Path

Visionaries emanate a soothing presence that ignites the spirit and elevates the mind. They hold a deep conviction in the realm of possibilities, enthusiastically illuminating the world. Their presence radiates an enchanting warmth, fostering hope and sparking creativity in those nearby. Much like beacons, they illuminate the darkness of others' doubts, leading the path toward a brighter tomorrow.

Consider Nelson Mandela, a figure whose aspiration for a harmonious South Africa emanated a profound sense of hope and strength. Even after spending decades behind bars, Mandela's indomitable spirit shone brightly, guiding the way toward healing and fairness. His presence radiated optimism, encouraging countless individuals to embrace the potential for a more luminous and inclusive tomorrow.

Another example is Oprah Winfrey, whose life journey from adversity to global influence stands as a beacon of hope for countless individuals. Oprah's conviction in the transformative nature of storytelling, coupled with her profound capacity to resonate with individuals emotionally, has motivated countless individuals to chase their aspirations and surmount their obstacles. Her hopeful and compassionate demeanor consistently inspires the imagination and ambitions of those she encounters.

Reflect on the impact of technology through the lens of its pioneers, such as Larry Page and Sergey Brin, the visionary founders of Google. Their groundbreaking perspective on structuring global information serves as a beacon in our digital era. Their unwavering optimism and enthusiasm for their mission not only transformed our access to information but also ignited a spark in a generation of tech entrepreneurs, encouraging them to explore the limits of possibility.

Visionaries such as Mandela, Winfrey, Page, and Brin exemplify a profound inner strength that empowers them to transcend challenges, inspiring and elevating those in their presence. Their enthusiasm and positive outlook cultivate a conviction in the remarkable, motivating individuals to reach their utmost potential. These beacons of optimism steer humanity toward a more radiant and hopeful future by shedding light on the journey ahead.

2. Igniting Potential: Unleashing the Power Within

Visionaries serve as the channels for the manifestation of potential. They have an extraordinary knack for awakening the hidden potential in those around them, perceiving deeper than the exterior to identify the unrecognized abilities of their peers and partners. This sense of empowerment encourages individuals to reach beyond their perceived limits, enabling them to venture beyond familiar boundaries and share their distinctive talents to benefit the collective. Collectively, this untapped potential has the power to transform landscapes and reshape the boundaries of possibility.

Reflect on Mahatma Gandhi, a figure who awakened the latent potential within countless individuals through his commitment to nonviolent resistance and civil disobedience. Gandhi's steadfast conviction in the efficacy of nonviolent resistance motivated innumerable souls to awaken and strive for India's liberation. His capacity to ignite the dormant potential in individuals illustrated how a profound thinker can inspire a shared journey and bring about remarkable transformation.

Consider Nelson Mandela's narrative. Mandela's aspiration for a racially inclusive South Africa motivated his followers to transcend their fears and diligently pursue justice and equality. His guidance inspired countless individuals to recognize their inherent capabilities and actively participate in the struggle against apartheid, culminating in the dismantling of that oppressive system and the creation of a democratic society.

In business, Steve Jobs exemplified a remarkable talent for recognizing the latent potential within individuals and encouraging them to transcend their limitations. At Apple, Jobs fostered a space where imagination and groundbreaking ideas flourished. His unwavering confidence in his team's potential resulted in innovative creations such as the iPhone and the iPad, fundamentally transforming the technology landscape.

In a comparable vein, Sheryl Sandberg, the COO of Facebook, has emerged as a guiding light of empowerment, especially for women navigating the complexities of the workplace. Her book, "Lean In," along with her commitment to gender equality, has motivated numerous women to seek leadership positions and embrace their complete potential. Sandberg's guidance has inspired countless individuals to transcend limitations and share their unique gifts with the world.

3. Liberators of Potential: Empowering Others to Rise

Through deliberate writing, those who envision a better world proclaim liberation. Visionary leaders act as catalysts for unleashing potential, understanding that each person, regardless of the challenges they encounter, has the ability to evolve into something extraordinary. They cultivate a space of affirmation and backing, allowing individuals to rise above their insecurities and pursue their dreams with vigor. They champion the vast possibilities inherent in human potential, cultivating a space where individuals can truly thrive.

Reflect on the profound influence of Nelson Mandela, whose guidance and commitment to equality inspired countless individuals to transcend the shackles of oppression. Mandela's steadfast conviction in the inherent potential of each South African ignited a transformative movement that dismantled apartheid and nurtured a more inclusive society. The capacity to unlock the inherent potential within individuals and communities serves as a profound illustration of the transformative essence of insightful leadership.

Consider Muhammad Yunus, the visionary behind Grameen Bank. Yunus transformed the understanding of microfinance by offering small loans to impoverished people who were often excluded from conventional banking systems. His conviction in the capacity of the underprivileged to forge improved futures for themselves inspired countless individuals to embark on entrepreneurial ventures, rise above poverty, and enrich their communities. Yunus' innovative perspective has significantly influenced economic growth and the enhancement of social well-being.

In business, one might reflect on Howard Schultz's leadership style, the former CEO of Starbucks. Schultz's focus on fostering a nurturing and inclusive workplace inspired employees to embrace their roles and play a vital part in the organization's achievements. His perspective on treating employees as collaborators nurtured an environment of cooperation and shared respect, allowing individuals to flourish and create with freedom.

In a parallel manner, Malala Yousafzai's commitment to promoting girls' education has inspired young women across the globe to chase their aspirations, even in the face of formidable obstacles. Malala's brave stance against oppressive forces and her steadfast conviction in the transformative power of education has motivated countless girls to pursue learning and realize their fullest potential.

These instances demonstrate that transformative leaders are essential in realizing individuals' full capacity. By cultivating a nurturing atmosphere, they inspire individuals to rise above their constraints and make significant contributions to the community. Those who see beyond the ordinary champion the vast possibilities inherent in human potential, initiating a profound impact that reshapes lives and fosters a brighter future for everyone.

4. Planting the Seeds of Ambition: Guiding Humanity Upward

They sow the seeds that blossom into routes leading to the cosmos. Visionaries serve as the cosmic cultivators of aspiration, inspiring and motivating one another toward greatness. They believe in humanity's potential, motivating others to aspire to their highest ambitions. Their vision serves as a beacon, illuminating a future that is richer and more fully realized in its potential.

Reflect on the case of Elon Musk, a figure who has sown the seeds of aspiration in the fields of space exploration and sustainable energy. His endeavors, including SpaceX and Tesla, seek to transform our perception of transportation and energy. Musk's conviction in humanity's capacity to transcend terrestrial constraints encourages individuals to envision grand aspirations and pursue what may appear unattainable.

Maya Angelou profoundly illustrates how impactful language and a steadfast dedication to social justice can ignite the aspirations of countless individuals across generations.

Angelou's poetry and autobiographical works invite readers to imagine a realm of equality and inspire them to strive to realize that vision. Her enduring influence is a beacon for those striving to foster significant transformation.

In the domain of scientific inquiry, Marie Curie's pioneering work in radioactivity has significantly expanded our understanding and possibilities in medicine and physics. Curie's unwavering commitment to her research and profound conviction in scientific inquiry's transformative potential established a foundation for future breakthroughs. Her contributions are a profound source of inspiration, encouraging scientists and researchers to transcend the limits of knowledge and innovation.

Visionaries such as Musk, Angelou, and Curie embody the qualities that position them as the architects of a more enlightened world. Their steadfast conviction in the potential of what could be, their bravery amidst challenges, and their commitment to advancing humanity compose a harmonious progression that motivates and elevates us collectively. Through the cultivation of ambition, they steer humanity towards an elevated future brimming with boundless possibilities.

Third Category: Innovative Action and Transformation

1. Alchemists of Adversity: From Chaos to Symphony

Obstacles serve simply as a canvas for the imaginative mind. Visionaries have an extraordinary ability to turn challenges into personal and collective development avenues. They view challenges not as failures but as opportunities to tap into their boundless creative potential. For them, challenges are seen as pathways to growth, transforming obstacles into canvases that inspire resilience and the artistry of innovation. They possess a remarkable ability to convert even the most chaotic situations into seamless successes.

Reflect on J.K. Rowling, who encountered countless rejections and personal challenges before the triumph of the Harry Potter series. Instead of succumbing to her challenges, Rowling transformed her hardships into a source of creativity, crafting an enchanting realm that resonates deeply with countless individuals. Her capacity to transform personal turmoil into a harmonious expression of creativity reflects a profound understanding of navigating challenges gracefully.

The trajectory of Elon Musk, along with Tesla and SpaceX, exemplifies this principle remarkably. Musk faced considerable financial and technical hurdles, grappling with the brink of bankruptcy for Tesla and a series of unsuccessful rocket launches for SpaceX. He perceived these challenges as avenues for growth and creativity. Through the strategic use of challenges, Musk has turned his obstacles into remarkable triumphs, guiding both enterprises to unprecedented heights.

Nelson Mandela's existence is a profound testament to the transformative power of overcoming challenges. Following 27 years of incarceration, Mandela reentered society with a profound vision for reconciliation and unity within South Africa. His extraordinary capacity to convert individual pain into a compelling catalyst for societal transformation has fostered a profound accomplishment that continues to motivate and uplift the global community.

Visionaries such as Rowling, Musk, and Mandela reveal that challenges transcend obstacles; they serve as gateways to creating something profoundly beautiful and transformative. Their ability to transform disorder into a harmonious achievement reveals the profound strength of an imaginative mind. By harnessing resilience and creativity, they create works of art that elevate and inspire the human spirit.

2. Breathing Life into the Mundane: The Empowerment Ethos

Through their insight, those visionaries grant meaning to the lifeless. Visionaries have the remarkable ability to transform the mundane into something truly exceptional. They perceive extraordinary potential in the simplest of objects or circumstances, possessing the ability to infuse them with vitality. By embracing creativity and fostering a spirit of empowerment, those with a profound vision transform the mundane into the remarkable.

Consider, for instance, Walt Disney, who recognized the profound possibilities for narrative and happiness within the most basic illustrations. His capacity to imagine a realm where animated figures could enchant and motivate led to a worldwide entertainment phenomenon. Disney's transformative power elevated ordinary illustrations into cherished symbols, infusing them with wonder and creativity.

In parallel, Elon Musk's ambitious vision for reshaping daily transportation has fundamentally altered the landscape of the automotive sector. By reimagining electric cars as practical novelties and appealing and feasible alternatives to conventional vehicles, Musk infused vitality into the ordinary and catalyzed a transformation toward sustainable transportation. Tesla's elegantly designed, high-performance electric vehicles have transformed our understanding and engagement with transportation, integrating them into a sustainable future vision.

Another illustration is Marie Kondo, whose methodology for organizing has reshaped perceptions of personal environments. Through her KonMari method, Kondo invites individuals to explore the transformative power of joy and simplicity in the art of organizing their possessions. Her approach to retaining only what ignites joy has inspired countless individuals to simplify their surroundings and discover tranquility and meaning within their living spaces.

Visionaries ignite a spark in others, encouraging them to perceive the world anew and uncover the extraordinary potential within the ordinary. They inspire people to engage actively and contribute to a movement that positively transforms the world. By envisioning a reality that transcends their own limitations and uplifts those around them, these individuals cultivate a profound ripple of innovation and change.

These instances illustrate that those with a visionary mindset can elevate the mundane into the remarkable. Their commitment to empowerment encourages individuals to recognize the latent possibilities within themselves and their surroundings, nurturing an environment ripe for innovation and advancement.

3. The Trailblazers: Challenging the Status Quo

They are trailblazers, unconventional thinkers determined in their quest to question and redefine the status quo through their approaches. Equipped with deep understanding and critical thought, they challenge the prevailing norms, examining established beliefs and transforming our perception of reality. Their inherent courage in challenging established norms, combined with a profound curiosity, compels them to extend the boundaries of conventional wisdom.

Reflect on the case of Steve Jobs, who transformed various sectors by questioning established norms. From personal computing to the world of music and mobile technology, Jobs relentlessly challenged the limits of possibility. His unwavering commitment to refined aesthetics and intuitive user experiences challenged conventional practices and established groundbreaking benchmarks for creativity.

Another visionary is Martin Luther King Jr., whose courageous stance on civil rights confronted deeply rooted societal conventions. His commitment to nonviolent resistance and his compelling oratory, exemplified by the legendary "I Have a Dream," transformed the struggle for equality and justice in America. The courage to challenge established norms through deep understanding and thoughtful analysis transformed societal dynamics and continues to motivate those who follow.

In the domain of scientific inquiry, Albert Einstein's theories fundamentally questioned and reshaped the established paradigms of physics. His theory of relativity challenged the long-standing Newtonian principles, reshaping the scientific community's understanding of space, time, and gravity. Einstein's insatiable curiosity and audacious spirit in challenging established norms paved the way for revolutionary discoveries that resonate within contemporary scientific thought.

In commerce, entities such as Airbnb and Uber have fundamentally transformed conventional sectors by redefining our perceptions of lodging and transit. These organizations have transformed market anticipations and established novel paradigms for delivering services through the strategic use of technology and creative business frameworks.

Visionaries such as Jobs, King, Einstein, and the pioneers of transformative enterprises embody the essence of innovation and groundbreaking thought. Their propensity to challenge established norms, along with a profound curiosity and keen insight, propels them to transform our comprehension of reality. By questioning established norms, they create opportunities for advancement and motivate others to expand their thinking beyond traditional boundaries.

4. Alchemists of the Modern Age: Transforming Reality

Visionaries embody the transformative thinkers of our time. Through their keen insight and unwavering determination, they reshape the world's raw elements into something profoundly remarkable and beneficial. In contrast to the general populace, who might find satisfaction in the status quo, those with a visionary mindset are perpetually on the quest for innovative methods to utilize nature's gifts for humanity's greater good. Their imaginative perspectives serve as the driving force for transformation in our society.

Reflect on Nikola Tesla's extraordinary impact. His groundbreaking advancements in electricity transformed the landscape of contemporary technology. Tesla's unwavering quest for innovative methods to utilize electrical energy culminated in creating alternating current (AC) systems, establishing the groundwork for the extensive dissemination of electricity. His profound understanding reshaped the fundamental aspects of nature into a dynamic and practical force that persistently serves the betterment of humanity.

Consider the case of Steve Jobs, a figure whose groundbreaking perspective on technology fundamentally altered various sectors. Jobs' capacity to transcend traditional technology uses and envision products that effortlessly blend into our everyday existence transformed our engagement with the digital realm. The iPhone exemplifies the convergence of communication, entertainment, and computing within a singular device, rendering it an essential instrument for countless individuals.

Individuals such as Elon Musk exemplify this principle in their pursuits. Musk's endeavors with SpaceX and Tesla illustrate his remarkable capacity to convert fundamental concepts into groundbreaking innovations. Musk's ability to imagine a future in which humanity thrives as a multi-planetary species, coupled with the widespread adoption of sustainable energy solutions, exemplifies his relentless pursuit of expanding the limits of possibility and transforming abstract ideas into concrete achievements.

In medicine, Dr. Jonas Salk's creation of a polio vaccine is a remarkable instance of transformative vision. Salk's groundbreaking method of employing inactivated virus particles to foster immunity revolutionized the fundamental science of virology, resulting in a monumental medical advancement that has largely eliminated polio across vast regions of the globe.

These instances illustrate that those with a visionary mindset, akin to contemporary alchemists, hold the creative wisdom and resolve to elevate the mundane into the remarkable. Their capacity to transcend the present circumstances and to create transformative solutions for the advancement of humanity propels progress and encourages us to expand the horizons of our imagination.

Fourth Category: Creating Impact and Legacy

1. The Harmonic Voice: Champions of Humanity

Their voice resonates as a symphony for the essence of humanity. Visionaries embody the essence of humanity, their voices weaving together a resonant and harmonious melody that echoes the principles of compassion and unity, transcending the barriers that divide us. They recognize that true advancement holds significance when it serves the collective, and they endeavor to connect diverse cultures while nurturing a sense of shared humanity. Through their advocacy for the enhancement of humanity and the promotion of global collaboration, they express their beliefs through their words and deeds.

Reflect on Malala Yousafzai, a figure whose commitment to girls' education surpasses cultural and national divides. Her voice resonates through her speeches and writings, advocating for a harmonious society where every child is afforded equal opportunities, irrespective of their origins. Malala's steadfast dedication to education and human rights has ignited a worldwide movement, advocating for the rights of countless individuals and envisioning a brighter future for everyone.

Consider Desmond Tutu, whose dedication to advancing human rights and fostering reconciliation has significantly shaped the fabric of global society. Tutu's endeavors to connect disparate cultures in the aftermath of apartheid in South Africa, particularly through initiatives such as the Truth and Reconciliation Commission, highlight his profound commitment to the betterment of humanity. His message of empathy, understanding, and togetherness has echoed across the globe, fostering a sense of shared healing and advancement.

Visionaries such as Oprah Winfrey exemplify this harmonious expression. Oprah's platform serves as a sanctuary for compassion, insight, and narrative, elevating many voices and experiences to the center stage. Her efforts in philanthropy and advocacy have inspired numerous individuals, fostering a profound sense of interconnectedness and collective human experience.

In environmental advocacy, Greta Thunberg's voice resonates profoundly as a compelling force in the struggle against climate change. Her heartfelt and insightful addresses inspire global leaders and individuals to unite in their efforts for the future of our planet. Thunberg's capacity to inspire individuals worldwide underscores the importance of a visionary in advocating for a collective and empathetic response to urgent global challenges.

2. Architects of Unity: Building Bridges of Collaboration

Visionaries serve as the builders of connection and harmony. They possess a remarkable ability to forge connections, nurturing collaboration that transcends borders and unites diverse cultures. They recognize that true innovation flourishes within a tapestry of diversity and interconnection. Barriers dissolve through the encouragement of collaboration, leading to a more cohesive global community. This nurtures a deeper exchange of ideas and enhances the sharing of resources and solutions across the globe.

Reflect on the contributions of Nelson Mandela and Desmond Tutu in the transformative era of post-apartheid South Africa. Their dedication to fostering understanding and harmony played a crucial role in mending profound societal rifts. The Truth and Reconciliation Commission catalyzed dialogue and understanding, fostering a healing journey that nurtured national unity and advancement. Their leadership serves as a testament to the capacity of visionaries to create connections that nurture a more cohesive and harmonious community.

Within corporate dynamics, Satya Nadella, the CEO of Microsoft, has championed the principles of collaboration and inclusivity. Through his guidance, Microsoft has cultivated strategic alliances with various technology firms, nurturing a cooperative atmosphere that propels innovation forward. Nadella's focus on fostering a growth mindset and embracing diverse viewpoints has cultivated an environment where creativity thrives, resulting in remarkable technological innovations.

The European Union serves as a compelling illustration of an initiative designed to foster economic collaboration and mitigate the potential for conflict. The EU's dedication to fostering unity and collaboration among its member states has been instrumental in driving economic growth, ensuring political stability, and promoting social progress throughout Europe. EU member nations' unity and joint endeavors exemplify the profound impact of working together to realize shared aspirations.

Within the sphere of environmental advocacy, entities such as the United Nations Environment Programme (UNEP) strive to cultivate a sense of global collaboration in tackling pressing environmental challenges. Through the collaboration of nations, scientists, and activists, UNEP fosters a rich dialogue and resource sharing, catalyzing unified efforts toward sustainability and conservation.

Influential figures such as Mandela, Tutu, and Nadella and entities like the EU and UNEP exemplify the importance of fostering collaborative connections to cultivate a more cohesive and innovative global landscape. By encouraging varied viewpoints and cultivating collaboration, they create a pathway toward a more promising future, one where shared advancement serves the interests of everyone.

3. Conductors of Progress: Ensuring Equitable Distribution

Visionaries serve as guides of advancement, facilitating the flow of innovation's rewards to all individuals, irrespective of their origins or situations. They seek to create a fair allocation of resources, aiming to prevent the advantages of advancement from being held by a select few. Their perspective transcends the individual, aspiring to cultivate an environment where all can flourish and realize their potential.

Reflect on Muhammad Yunus's contributions and the establishment of Grameen Bank. Yunus understood the importance of fair access to financial resources and was a trailblazer in the idea of microfinance. By providing small loans to those in need without the burden of collateral, Yunus enabled countless individuals to transcend the limitations of poverty and reclaim their agency. His contributions have catalyzed significant economic growth and highlighted the necessity of making the fruits of advancement available to everyone.

Consider the impactful initiatives led by Melinda Gates via the Bill & Melinda Gates Foundation. The foundation's initiatives emphasize the importance of global health, education, and economic empowerment, aiming to guarantee that the fruits of innovation and advancement extend to the most underserved communities. Their endeavors to eliminate diseases such as polio and enhance access to education and healthcare reflect a profound dedication to the just allocation for the resources.

Figures such as Nelson Mandela exemplify this principle beautifully. Mandela's struggle against apartheid and his aspiration for a racially inclusive society stemmed from the conviction that every individual is entitled to equal opportunities. His guidance in formulating policies that fostered social and economic fairness created a more equitable and cohesive South Africa.

Within the realm of technology, organizations such as Google are undertaking efforts to close the gap in digital access. Initiatives such as Google Fiber seek to bridge the digital divide by delivering high-speed internet access to marginalized communities, thereby fostering a more equitable distribution of technological progress across society. This dedication to fair access to technology fosters a landscape where educational, employment, and innovative opportunities are more inclusive for all.

These examples demonstrate how visionaries serve as orchestrators of advancement, facilitating the fair distribution of innovation's rewards. Their commitment to fostering inclusive systems and equitably distributing resources lays the foundation for a reality where every individual can flourish.

4. Sculpting Tomorrows: Decisive Action for a Brighter Future

Decisive in action, visionaries sculpt the present to create future possibilities. They embody a resolute leadership style, skillfully translating their insights into concrete outcomes. They embrace the necessity of making difficult decisions, recognizing that decisive action is crucial for crafting a more promising future. Their bravery and vision empower them to traverse the ambiguities of today while establishing the foundation for a more promising future. The decisions made in the present resonate profoundly, shaping the fabric of future generations.

Reflect on Franklin D. Roosevelt's leadership during the Great Depression. Roosevelt's resolute measures, particularly introducing the New Deal, sought to deliver prompt assistance, stimulate economic revival, and instigate financial reforms. His capacity to navigate difficult choices amidst significant obstacles shaped a more promising future for America, establishing the groundwork for enduring prosperity and stability.

Indra Nooyi's leadership as CEO of PepsiCo is a testament to the power of decisive action in corporate dynamics. Nooyi embraced courageous decisions to broaden PepsiCo's product range and prioritize healthier alternatives, recognizing consumers' evolving desires. Her insightful perspective and resolute choices catalyzed a profound transformation within the company, securing its ongoing evolution and significance in a challenging marketplace.

Consider the impactful work of Wangari Maathai, who established the Green Belt Movement as a profound expression of environmental advocacy. Maathai's impactful initiatives in advocating for reforestation and sustainable development in Kenya confronted essential environmental and societal challenges. Her bravery and vision played a crucial role in environmental preservation and uplifted communities, fostering a profound legacy of transformative impact.

Influential figures such as Roosevelt, Nooyi, and Maathai exemplify the importance of decisive action to forge a more promising future. Their capacity to embrace bold decisions despite the unknown empowers them to leave a profound legacy and illuminate the path for those who will follow. By transforming vision into tangible action, they shape a reality that resonates with advancement and potential.

5. The Pioneers: Leaving a Legacy of Innovation

Visionaries serve as pioneers, crafting unique routes characterized by the imprints of innovation. They guide others, shedding light on various paths through deliberate actions and thoughtful choices. Their achievements forge an enduring legacy, crafting a story that will undoubtedly resonate with future generations. They foster a profound legacy of growth and enhancement.

Reflect on the groundbreaking essence embodied by the Wright brothers, Orville and Wilbur Wright. Their unwavering quest for powered flight culminated in the inaugural successful airplane, transforming transportation and inviting humanity to explore the vastness of the skies. The enduring influence of their groundbreaking ideas catalyzes progress in aviation and aerospace, underscoring the significant contributions of visionary thinkers.

Consider the case of Marie Curie, whose pioneering work in radioactivity established a crucial basis for many scientific progressions. Her groundbreaking discoveries garnered her two Nobel Prizes and laid the foundation for future advancements in medicine, physics, and chemistry. Curie's enduring legacy of innovation profoundly shapes scientific inquiry and provides inspiration for countless researchers globally.

In the realm of technology, Google's creators, Larry Page and Sergey Brin, embody the essence of true innovation. Their development of a formidable search engine revolutionized our approach to accessing and organizing information. Google's influence reaches well beyond mere search capabilities, fostering advancements across diverse domains, including artificial intelligence, digital advertising, and self-driving technology. Their pioneering spirit leaves an indelible mark, reflected in their established enterprise's expansive reach and profound impact.

Visionaries such as the Wright brothers, Curie, Page, and Brin illustrate how pioneers can profoundly influence the world around them. Their imaginative traces carve out fresh routes, guiding others toward advancement and originality. Through courageous decisions and transformative actions, these trailblazers forge a legacy that influences the future and propels ongoing progress.

In Summary, visionaries are rare yet possess an unparalleled influence. Masters of this magnificent symphony navigate through these traits, crafting a stunning melody that inspires and stirs the hearts of all who hear it. Their light illuminates the path to a more promising future, ensuring the world is improved for those who come after them.

Fifth Category: Visionary Leadership and Collaboration

1. Architects of Harmony: Bridging the Divide

They foster relationships in spaces that were previously marked by separation. Visionaries craft the blueprint for balance and understanding. They understand the complex connections that unite everything and endeavor to bridge ideas that might initially appear unrelated. They hold a viewpoint that goes beyond basic human needs, deeply anchored in understanding a broader planetary reality.

Reflect on the contributions of Wangari Maathai, the visionary behind the Green Belt Movement. Maathai's endeavors in environmental conservation and the advocacy for women's rights created a profound connection between ecological sustainability and social justice. Her initiative fostered a dual impact, advancing reforestation efforts in Kenya while simultaneously empowering women, granting them the chance to actively engage and uplift their communities. Maathai's comprehensive perspective intertwined ecological and societal issues, crafting a cohesive framework for enduring progress.

Consider the leadership of the Dalai Lama, whose insights highlight the profound significance of compassion and the intricate web of our interconnectedness. The Dalai Lama's commitment to nonviolence and global harmony goes beyond cultural and religious divides, nurturing a profound sense of unity among various communities. His viewpoint on the interwoven fabric of existence fosters comprehension and collaboration, motivating shared advancement.

Elon Musk's ambitious vision for a multi-planetary existence through SpaceX intricately links humanity's future with the profound exploration of space. Musk's initiatives emphasize the profound relationship between human civilization's survival and progress and the exploration of new frontiers, illustrating the deep connection between technological innovation and the sustainability of our planet.

Visionaries such as Maathai, the Dalai Lama, and Musk illustrate the profound impact of those who cultivate harmony, fostering connections of understanding and collaboration. Their guidance, innovative spirit, and steadfast conviction in a more promising future motivate us to unlock our true potential and play a role in shaping a luminous tomorrow. By embodying these traits, visionaries take on the role of orchestrators in a magnificent symphony of advancement, leading us toward a more cohesive and interconnected existence.

2. Sculptors of Culture: Shaping Societies of Tomorrow

Visionaries profoundly influence the core of our cultural landscape. They mold the structures of industry and impact the essence of society. This creative energy shapes the cultural landscape, guiding the way for those who will come after us. They grasp the profound relationship between enterprise and societal values, striving to develop offerings and experiences that enrich our existence.

Reflect on the profound influence Steve Jobs has had on contemporary culture. Jobs' groundbreaking perspective on Apple reshaped technology and our engagement with the world around us. His focus on design, simplicity, and user experience established new benchmarks for consumer electronics, shaping the cultural environment of the digital era. The iPhone has emerged as a fundamental element of our everyday existence, profoundly influencing how we communicate, engage in entertainment, and conduct our professional lives.

Walt Disney serves as a prime illustration, as his imaginative works have profoundly influenced and shaped the fabric of global culture. The artistry of storytelling in animation, as envisioned by Disney, has given rise to cherished characters and magical realms, nurturing a profound sense of wonder and delight. The Disney brand embodies the essence of imagination and creativity, influencing countless generations and intricately weaving itself into the cultural tapestry of entertainment.

Influential figures such as Oprah Winfrey significantly shape the fabric of our culture. Through her extensive media presence, Oprah has shaped public conversation, fostered understanding, and advocated for societal transformation. Her capacity to engage with audiences and tackle significant issues has influenced societal values and motivated countless individuals to pursue improvement.

Coco Chanel transformed the landscape of women's fashion, ushering in an era of modernity and comfort that defied conventional standards. Chanel's creations transcended mere fashion; they catalyzed a profound empowerment of women, playing a pivotal role in reshaping cultural narratives around gender roles and societal norms.

These instances illustrate that those with foresight are the architects of societal norms. Their creative insights shape industries and societal norms, crafting products and experiences that enrich our existence. Through a profound comprehension of the intricate relationship between enterprise and societal values, insightful leaders pave the way for those to come, fostering a more dynamic and enriched existence.

3. The Orchestrators of Progress: Harnessing Power for Humanity's Benefit

Visionaries serve as the architects of advancement. They possess a deep awareness of the resources at their disposal and demonstrate an adeptness in maximizing their potential. These visionary individuals manipulate the forces of nature for the advancement of humanity, leading us into uncharted territories. Possessing a profound sense of foresight, they can perceive what has yet to materialize and catalyze solutions that positively influence the course of history. They understand the delicate balance of reciprocity, recognizing that advancement requires sacrifice while ensuring that the rewards significantly surpass the investments made.

Reflect on Bill Gates' endeavors. Through the Bill & Melinda Gates Foundation, Gates has utilized his resources and impact to tackle pressing global health issues. Gates' efforts to eliminate diseases such as polio and malaria reflect a profound commitment to advancing humanity's well-being. Through the strategic utilization of financial assets, advancements in technology, and collaborative international alliances, Gates has profoundly influenced health outcomes on a global scale.

Another illustration is Elon Musk, whose endeavors with Tesla and SpaceX embody the intricate design of advancement. Musk's aspirations regarding sustainable energy and space exploration have catalyzed remarkable progress in electric vehicles and aerospace innovation. His profound grasp of resources and their innovative application has transcended conventional limits, fostering advantages beyond immediate commercial triumph.

Muhammad Yunus has catalyzed advancement in social entrepreneurship through the innovative approach of microfinance. Through the provision of modest loans to those marginalized by conventional banking systems, Yunus enabled individuals to establish their own enterprises and enhance their financial circumstances. This groundbreaking method has significantly impacted the alleviation of poverty and the advancement of economic growth across the globe.

Visionaries such as Gates, Musk, and Yunus illustrate that the architects of advancement are those who grasp the entirety of available resources and possess the insight to utilize them effectively for the collective benefit. Their creative approaches and insightful vision empower them to traverse the intricate landscape of advancement, guaranteeing that the advantages they generate significantly surpass the associated costs.

These thinkers remind us that genuine advancement is realized through a nuanced interplay of creativity, ingenuity, and dedication to humanity's welfare. The strategic use of power aimed at collective well-being creates a pathway toward a future filled with limitless possibilities, ensuring that the advantages are accessible to everyone.

4. Champions of Progress: The Vanguard of Civilization

Visionaries embody the essence of advancement. They journey with advancement, embracing fresh vistas to uncover every possibility. They illuminate the path, inspiring individuals to welcome the trials of change and explore innovative concepts. They embody the essence of liberation, keenly recognizing that progress thrives in environments that cultivate original ideas and bold perspectives. Their steadfast optimism and strength drive humanity forward into a brighter future.

Reflect on the profound impact of Martin Luther King Jr., whose aspirations for civil rights and equality represented a transformative chapter in the narrative of American history. This leader's dedication to nonviolent resistance and compelling rhetoric galvanized a nation to face systemic injustice and pursue a more just society. His steadfast optimism and tenacity in confronting challenges made him a genuine advocate for advancement.

In the realm of commerce, reflect on the groundbreaking contributions of Jeff Bezos, the visionary behind Amazon. Bezos transformed the retail landscape through his pioneering approach to e-commerce and cutting-edge supply chain strategies. His openness to venture into uncharted territories and reshape conventional business frameworks has significantly influenced worldwide trade, positioning Amazon as a technological and logistical advancement leader.

Another illustration is Malala Yousafzai, whose commitment to girls' education persistently confronts and reshapes societal norms. In the face of life-threatening challenges, Malala embodies resilience and hope, passionately advocating for every girl's fundamental right to education. Her leadership and courage make her a beacon of progress, motivating countless individuals to champion human rights and foster social transformation.

Visionaries such as King, Bezos, and Malala embody the essence of those who champion progress. They represent the core of progress, steering humanity toward a more luminous tomorrow. Their bravery in questioning established norms and dedication to fostering groundbreaking ideas drive societal progress. Through the acceptance of change and advocacy for liberation, these trailblazers motivate us to aspire toward greater achievements and play a part in creating a brighter future.

Sixth Category: Personal and Societal Growth

1. Weaving the Tapestry of Balance: Champions of Reciprocity

Visionaries embody the essence of mutual exchange. They possess an innate awareness of the universe's equilibrium, recognizing that every gain is met with an equal measure of push or loss. They advocate for a harmonious relationship between human advancement and preserving our environment, emphasizing that true progress should not compromise our planet's and future generations' well-being.

Through their insights, they promote equilibrium and guide others in understanding how progress can be mindful.

Reflect on the contributions of Jane Goodall, whose pioneering studies on chimpanzees are intertwined with an unwavering dedication to conservation efforts. Goodall's commitment to the environment transcends her scientific achievements. She advocates for a harmonious path toward human advancement, highlighting the importance of safeguarding our natural environments and the rich tapestry of life they support. Through her foundation, she fosters awareness and motivates individuals to embrace sustainable practices, harmonizing development with conservation.

Consider the impactful leadership of environmental activist Wangari Maathai. As the visionary behind the Green Belt Movement, Maathai championed the principles of reforestation and sustainable land management in Kenya. Her efforts transcended mere environmental concerns, fostering a sense of agency within communities, especially among women, to engage meaningfully in the stewardship of their surroundings. Maathai's perspective on the harmonious connection between humanity and the natural world has profoundly influenced our understanding of ecological and social sustainability.

In business, Yvon Chouinard, the founder of Patagonia, has passionately championed environmental stewardship. Patagonia's business model embodies a profound commitment to sustainability, seamlessly combining recycled materials and the support of grassroots environmental initiatives. Chouinard's leadership exemplifies the potential for businesses to flourish by embracing ecological harmony and mutual respect.

Visionaries such as Goodall, Maathai, and Chouinard embody the essence of advocates for mutual respect and interconnectedness. They recognize that true advancement requires a commitment to sustainability, ensuring that our planet's health and future generations' welfare are integral to every step forward. Through their commitment to equilibrium and mindful progress, these thought leaders craft a narrative of unity that paves the way for a more luminous and sustainable tomorrow for everyone.

2. The Spark of Joy: Innovators of Delight

Visionaries ignite the essence of joy. Their creations are deeply appreciated; they imbue every wonder in the universe with a profound sense of joy and celebration. They embody the intrinsic human longing for beauty and artistic expression, immersing themselves in every opportunity for engagement and exploration. Emerging from their innovative designs are streams of joy, enriching lives and elevating communities.

Reflect on Walt Disney's profound influence. His creative genius has inspired countless individuals and fostered happiness through the establishment of Disney parks and the artistry of animated films. Disney's dedication to crafting enchanting experiences for individuals of all ages has revolutionized entertainment, fulfilling aspirations and igniting happiness across the globe. His enduring legacy evokes a sense of wonder and joy that resonates through the ages, inspiring countless individuals.

Another illustration is Steve Jobs, whose approach to design at Apple emphasized the harmonious blend of aesthetic appeal and practical utility. The elegant and intuitive design of Apple products, encompassing everything from iPhones to MacBooks, has fostered a sense of delight and ease for users. Jobs' meticulous focus and unwavering dedication to aesthetic brilliance have transformed ordinary technology into a source of profound joy.

Visionaries such as Marie Kondo embody this principle beautifully. Kondo's method of decluttering, focused on retaining only what ignites a sense of joy, has profoundly reshaped individuals' relationships with their belongings. Her approach has enabled individuals to cultivate environments fostering joy and serenity, enriching their well-being.

In architecture, Antoni Gaudí's creations in Barcelona exemplify how innovative design can evoke profound joy. Gaudí's distinctive and imaginative architectural approach, exemplified by masterpieces such as the Sagrada Família and Park Güell, envelops the city in enchantment and aesthetic allure. His creations persist in enchanting and motivating individuals from across the globe.

Their groundbreaking designs and creations infuse everyday life with joy and a sense of celebration, transforming the mundane into something extraordinary. Their contributions underscore the vital role that beauty and artistic expression play in cultivating well-being and nurturing a sense of community. Through the expression of their insights and enthusiasm, they contribute to a world that is both more joyful and fulfilling.

3. Architects of Abundance: Elevating the Quality of Life

Visionaries act as architects of abundance, foreseeing a future where all individuals' quality of life is elevated. Their creations transcend the boundaries of exclusivity; they hold a sincere conviction that the remarkable ought to be within reach for all individuals. They believe a rising tide lifts all boats and works towards a reality where everyone can flourish.

Reflect on Muhammad Yunus's contributions through Grameen Bank. Yunus' groundbreaking strategy in microfinance has empowered countless individuals to access the financial resources necessary for entrepreneurship and enhanced their quality of life. His aspiration to democratize financial services for the underprivileged has significantly enhanced the quality of life for numerous individuals, illustrating that wealth can be distributed broadly.

Consider the influence of affordable healthcare initiatives championed by individuals such as Paul Farmer, co-founder of Partners In Health. Farmer's dedication to delivering exceptional healthcare to marginalized communities in Haiti and beyond underscores a profound conviction: that the right to outstanding medical care should transcend economic barriers and be accessible to all, not just the affluent. His contributions have profoundly enhanced numerous individuals' well-being and overall quality of life.

Through his initiatives, Bill Gates seeks to address disparities in technology access, striving to create a more equitable digital landscape via the Bill & Melinda Gates Foundation. By providing technology and digital literacy initiatives, Gates aims to foster an equitable distribution of technological progress's advantages, ensuring that individuals from diverse socioeconomic backgrounds can partake in these benefits. His vision embraces a reality where technology catalyzes empowerment and elevation for all individuals.

Visionaries such as these illustrate that genuine advancement embraces inclusivity and extends its reach profoundly. Their dedication to enhancing the human experience for everyone generates a profound ripple effect, fostering abundance and potential for all. By creating inclusive systems and solutions, they cultivate an environment where each person can flourish.

4. Reaching for the Stars: Embracing the Uncharted

Visionaries advance into uncharted territories, gazing at the infinite expanse above. These timeless seekers direct their attention toward the unexplored realms of what lies ahead, fueled by an insatiable curiosity and an ambition to expand the limits of understanding. They perceive challenges not as barriers but as gateways to explore uncharted territories and unveil fresh potentials. Their relentless pursuit of understanding drives themselves and those in their orbit toward unexplored territories of creativity and advancement.

Reflect on the groundbreaking essence embodied by Elon Musk. Musk's endeavors with SpaceX and Tesla illustrate his relentless pursuit of the unknown. His aspiration to expand human existence across multiple planets and transform transportation through electric vehicles challenges our current understanding, consistently forging new paths forward. Musk's unwavering quest for knowledge and audacious aspirations motivate individuals to unite in their pursuit of the cosmos.

Consider the enduring impact of Amelia Earhart, whose bold ventures into aviation not only shattered records but also ignited the aspirations of countless future pilots. Earhart's relentless drive to transcend the limits of aviation and her aspiration to circle the globe exemplified her steadfast dedication to exploring the unknown. Her groundbreaking accomplishments serve as a beacon for those who dare to question conventional norms.

In scientific exploration, Marie Curie's pioneering investigations into radioactivity led her to uncharted domains. Curie's unwavering quest for understanding and her passion for revealing new scientific realities drove her to achieve breakthroughs that continue to profoundly influence the fields of medicine and physics. Her legacy stands as a profound reminder of the transformative potential that lies in welcoming the unknown on the journey toward innovation.

Trailblazers such as Musk, Earhart, and Curie reveal that those who boldly explore uncharted territories brighten the journey toward advancement. Their relentless pursuit of knowledge and unwavering desire to uncover the unknown propel humanity into uncharted territories, motivating us to aspire to greatness and delve into the boundless opportunities that await us beyond the horizon.

5. Weaving the Threads of Time: Seers of the Future

Visionaries intricately intertwine the fabric of time. They draw wisdom from the intricate weave of history, recognizing that the past not only informs the present but also molds the future. This distinctive perspective allows for anticipating trends far ahead and creating solutions that will hold significance for many years ahead. It could be argued that they resemble time travelers, extracting wisdom from the past to forge a more promising future.

Reflect on Steve Jobs' contributions. His deep insight into historical and technological progress and consumer tendencies enabled him to anticipate the evolution of personal computing and digital media. Jobs' capacity to intertwine the fabric of time led to groundbreaking creations such as the iPhone and the iPod, which revolutionized industries and molded the digital realm for future generations.

Consider the groundbreaking contributions of John Maynard Keynes, whose profound understanding during the Great Depression led to the formulation of macroeconomic theories that resonate within contemporary economic policy. Keynes's capacity to extract insights from historical occurrences and anticipate forthcoming economic dilemmas has created an enduring impact, steering decision-makers during periods of fiscal turmoil.

In environmental conservation, Rachel Carson's seminal work "Silent Spring" utilized historical data and research to illuminate the impending threats posed by pesticide use. Carson's profound insight and capacity to link historical practices with their future environmental consequences ignited the contemporary environmental movement, resulting in notable policy transformations and heightened public consciousness regarding ecological matters.

Visionaries such as Jobs, Keynes, and Carson illustrate that the fabric of time is woven through a deep comprehension of the complex relationships that link the past, present, and future. The capacity to harness historical insights while forecasting future developments empowers the creation of enduring solutions. By accepting their position as foresighted individuals, these pioneers lead humanity toward a more aware and enlightened future.

The Visionary's Mind: Unraveling the Mysteries Behind Civilizational Progress

The focus should extend beyond merely producing new ideas; instead, creative vision acts as a crucial psychological element shaping civilizations' course. It resides in the awareness of those who embody a remarkable blend of characteristics, some of which may appear mysterious, yet they profoundly impact the world around them. Exploring the depths of the visionary's mind reveals the mysterious origin of their influence. Structured around essential themes, we will delve into the complex dimensions that characterize visionary minds:

First Category: Visionary Traits and Motivations:

1. Resilient Optimism: The Builders of Progress

Builders of Progress: Creative thinking is a tool for those who mold advancement, yet simplicity seldom brightens their path. They exemplify steadfast positivity, showcasing incredible resilience and a unique capacity to bounce back from adversity. This optimism goes beyond simple stubbornness; it reflects a deep-seated conviction in the innate ability to surmount obstacles, regardless of the difficulties encountered. Their steadfast positivity emanates, drawing in those nearby and fostering a shared sense of strength as they confront the unknown challenges that lie ahead.

Reflect on Thomas Edison, whose unwavering positivity and determination culminated in creating the electric lightbulb. Despite countless setbacks, Edison profoundly asserted, "I have not failed." I have recently discovered 10,000 methods that prove ineffective. His capacity to uphold an affirmative perspective and extract lessons from every challenge embodies the essence of resilient optimism. This steadfast conviction in his vision drove him onward and motivated those in his vicinity to endure challenges.

Visionaries such as Nelson Mandela exemplify a profound and unwavering sense of hopefulness in the face of adversity. Even after 27 years of confinement, Mandela's unwavering faith in justice and equality remained steadfast. His unwavering strength and optimistic perspective were instrumental in breaking apartheid and nurturing reconciliation in South Africa. Mandela's unwavering hope carried him through his challenges and sparked a shared sense of strength among those who rallied behind him.

2. Foresight and Leadership: The Enigma of the Forerunner

Forerunner of Civilization: The driving force behind civilization has often been the imaginative insight of its leaders, propelling societies into unexplored realms. Wherever one looks for this creative vision, it emerges as the precursor to the advancement of civilization. Throughout history, civilization has been guided by a select few whose innovative thinking and keen awareness allowed them to remain in front of the collective consciousness.

The visionary leader presents a fascinating intricacy, a character enveloped in multiple dimensions of enigma. Those who nurture a visionary mindset possess an extraordinary ability to see beyond the present moment, skillfully recognizing emerging trends and societal shifts with uncanny foresight. This insight empowers individuals to lead their audience into uncharted territories, sometimes leaving them bewildered by the visionary's seemingly erratic shifts.

Reflect on Winston Churchill's leadership throughout World War II's tumultuous period. Churchill's remarkable insight and steadfast determination were instrumental in navigating Britain through a profoundly challenging era. His capacity to grasp the deeper significance of the conflict and unite the populace through his compelling oratory illustrated the mystery of transformative leadership. Churchill's remarkable insight and strategic brilliance allowed him to make pivotal decisions that influenced the trajectory of history.

Consider the transformative leadership exemplified by Jeff Bezos, the visionary behind Amazon. Bezos' keen insight into the possibilities of e-commerce and his remarkable capacity to foresee market dynamics have elevated Amazon to extraordinary levels of success. While often perplexing to others, his strategic vision has undeniably catalyzed transformative changes across retail, cloud computing, and beyond.

These examples reveal that the mystery of the forerunner resides in their capacity to perceive and traverse the future with a visionary understanding. Their leadership, characterized by depth and vision, navigates societies through unexplored realms and influences the course of civilization.

3. The Inner Flame: Uncovering the Hidden Layers of Motivation

Desire for Self-Expression: The yearning for authentic expression of the self. The inner flame of the visionary can often be complex and shrouded in shadows. Among the most powerful motivations is an unquenchable thirst for self-expression—an enthusiasm for leaving a mark on the world and transcending the constraints of convention. This motivation is revealed through various avenues, from creative endeavors to groundbreaking scientific advancements.

Reflect on Vincent van Gogh, whose profound passion for self-expression propelled him to produce some of the most renowned artworks in history. In the face of mental health challenges and societal alienation, van Gogh's profound urge to convey his distinctive perspective drove him to create iconic works such as "Starry Night" and "Sunflowers." While not entirely recognized during his era, his contributions have evolved into a profound illustration of how self-expression can influence and transform the cultural milieu.

Consider the case of Elon Musk's profound motivation for innovation and authentic self-expression, which has catalyzed remarkable progress in technology and space exploration. Musk's endeavors, including Tesla and SpaceX, embody his ambition to challenge limits and reshape the realm of possibility. His unwavering commitment to his vision, fueled by an intrinsic desire to create meaningful change, consistently inspires and reshapes entire industries.

These examples demonstrate that the intrinsic drive for self-expression is a profound catalyst for those envisioning new possibilities. It ignites their fervor to transcend traditional boundaries and leave a meaningful mark on the world. By revealing and accepting this concealed aspect of motivation, those with insight can direct their creative energy toward profound accomplishments.

4. The Power of Incentive: Profit Motive as a Driver

Inspiration for Personal Initiative: Motivation rooted in personal gain can be a powerful catalyst for innovative thinking. However, the term "profit" transcends mere financial gain; it embodies the deep satisfaction derived from bringing an idea to fruition, realizing a lifelong aspiration, or acknowledging one's impact on the world. The interplay of intrinsic motivation and the allure of external rewards cultivates a dynamic force that propels innovation forward.

Reflect on Steve Jobs' narrative and the inception of Apple. Jobs' motivation transcended mere financial gain; it was rooted in a profound desire to innovate and develop transformative products that would reshape the world. The profound fulfillment derived from witnessing his vision transform into groundbreaking creations such as the iPhone and Mac served as a compelling motivation. The interplay between intrinsic motivation and the extrinsic validation of acknowledgment and achievement propelled Jobs' unwavering quest for groundbreaking innovation.

Consider the case of Elon Musk, whose initiatives like SpaceX and Tesla are propelled by a profound aspiration to transform both space exploration and the sustainable energy landscape. Musk's pursuit of profit is intricately linked to his desire to influence human progress. The pursuit of success, recognition, and financial rewards pales in comparison to the profound fulfillment derived from advancing technology and addressing the pressing challenges of our world. This powerful amalgamation of intentions propels Musk's relentless pursuit of innovation and advancement.

These instances illustrate that the true strength of incentive emerges from the harmonious blend of intrinsic and extrinsic rewards. Innovators harness this collaboration to ignite their imaginative pursuits, expanding the limits of possibility and fostering profound transformation.

5. The Power of the Alluring Motive: Motivation for Excellence

Power of Attractive Motives: The best way to arouse an individual's motivation to excel is by presenting an important and compelling motive. The motives evoked must create a related desire that drives personal initiative. People are best motivated to do their best when they are driven by inner motives that compel them to take ownership of their success. Attractive motives create a magnetic pull, drawing people toward excellence. Fueled by the pleasure of achievement and contribution, this intrinsic drive is far more powerful than any external pressures or coercive measures.

Consider Google's 20% time policy, which allows employees to spend a portion of their work hours on projects they are passionate about. This initiative taps into employees' intrinsic motivation, fostering creativity and innovation. The freedom to explore personal interests and the opportunity to contribute to meaningful projects create a powerful allure, driving employees to excel. Many of Google's successful products, like Gmail and AdSense, originated from this motivational approach.

Another example is the open-source software movement, where developers contribute to projects out of passion and a desire to create something valuable for the community. The intrinsic motivation to collaborate, learn, and achieve collective goals drives developers to contribute their best efforts without the need for external incentives. This powerful drive has led to the creation of robust and widely used software like Linux, which continues to evolve and improve through the contributions of motivated individuals.

These examples illustrate that alluring motives have the power to inspire personal initiative and a sense of ownership. Visionaries can unleash individuals' full potential by tapping into intrinsic desires and creating a magnetic pull toward excellence, driving innovation and progress.[9]

Second Category: Empowering Others and Recognizing Efforts:

1. Rewarding Initiative: The Unseen Engine of Advancement

Advancement of Civilization: The progression of society is often rooted in the enduring principles that encourage the recognition of individual effort through meaningful rewards. Throughout history, societies that have achieved remarkable

---

[9] By harnessing the power of boundless service, rewarding positive motivations, fostering creativity through supportive policies, and understanding the power of intrinsic motivation, we can empower individuals and civilizations to reach their full potential.

progress have consistently fostered an environment where individual initiative is recognized and valued. Creativity flourishes in an environment where people are empowered to embrace uncertainty, explore unconventional ideas, and share their distinct abilities. This subtle yet profound system of rewards serves as the hidden force propelling the progress of societies.

Reflect on the Renaissance, an era characterized by a vibrant blossoming of artistic expression, scientific inquiry, and cultural advancement across Europe. This period was marked by a system of support where creators, scholars, and intellectuals were acknowledged and nurtured for their valuable insights and innovations. Visionaries such as Leonardo da Vinci and Michelangelo transcended the limitations of their disciplines, driven by the recognition and encouragement of their creativity and initiative. This deep-seated admiration for innovation ignited an era of remarkable advancement.

Consider Silicon Valley, a prime illustration of a global epicenter for technological innovation. The prevailing ethos of celebrating individual initiative and a readiness to take risks has fostered a landscape in which startups and entrepreneurs can flourish. Organizations like Google and Apple embody a culture that honors innovative concepts and daring endeavors. The prevailing ethos of innovation has catalyzed extraordinary technological progress, leaving a significant imprint on the global economic landscape.

These instances illustrate that recognizing and rewarding initiative plays an essential role in society's progress. Creating a space acknowledging and celebrating individual initiative allows communities to tap into their members' vast capabilities, propelling ongoing advancement and creativity.

2. Boundless Service: The Power of the "Extra Mile" Attitude

Extra Mile Attitude: A mindset that embraces the journey beyond the ordinary. Those with a creative vision transcend boundaries and limitations. They continually surpass what is anticipated, putting in additional effort to amplify their influence. Their intrinsic motivation is driven by an unwavering commitment to serve others. They recognize that genuine advancement frequently demands a selfless commitment and an openness to engage beyond mere obligations.

Reflect on Mahatma Gandhi, who transcended his duties to motivate and guide a nation in its quest for independence. Gandhi's unwavering dedication to nonviolence and selfless service embodies the essence of going above and beyond. His unwavering commitment to elevate and bring together the people of India, frequently at significant personal cost, establishes a benchmark of leadership and altruism that remains a source of inspiration.

Consider Howard Schultz, the previous CEO of Starbucks. Schultz's commitment to going above and beyond is evident in his dedication to fostering an inclusive and supportive workplace. He was at the forefront of initiatives that included extending healthcare benefits to part-time employees and advocating for the ethical sourcing of coffee. Schultz's dedication to transcending mere obligations cultivated an environment of compassion and empowerment at Starbucks and played a pivotal role in the company's achievements.

This commitment to going above and beyond sets apart those who envision a greater future from the ordinary. They embrace every avenue available, consistently welcoming challenges and seizing opportunities to create a meaningful impact. They recognize that harnessing their initiative is essential for realizing their fullest potential and inspiring others to embark on a similar journey.

3. Rewarding the Best: The Foundation of Great Civilizations

Recognizing Excellence: Thriving communities arise from appreciating and encouraging constructive motivations. The societal appreciation for merit and creativity fundamentally influences progression. Consider, for example, the period of the Medici family, who championed artists and thinkers during the Renaissance. Their support cultivated an environment conducive to constructive development and shared efforts, leading to an extraordinary increase in innovation and progress.

Companies like Google and Microsoft exemplify remarkable advancements in today's world by cultivating atmospheres that prioritize creativity and proactive engagement. Google's "20% time" initiative empowers employees to allocate a segment of their workweek to pursue personal projects, creating innovative products like Gmail and Google News. This policy exemplifies the profound impact of fostering personal initiative and creativity on catalyzing innovation and achieving success.

Reward systems ought to transcend mere acknowledgment of individual accomplishments; they should foster a continuous cycle that inspires further contributions and nurtures personal growth. By acknowledging and fostering positive motivations, communities, and organizations celebrate individual achievements and create structures that promote ongoing development and shared success.

This methodology fosters an environment where creativity flourishes. It allows advancement advantages to be distributed equitably, establishing a strong basis for flourishing societies.

4. The Spark Within: Encouraging the Pursuit of Creative Vision

Fostering Aspiration: The creative vision should not be regarded as an exclusive talent reserved for only a privileged minority. Rather, it ought to be perceived as a deep yearning, a delicate spark poised to be kindled within each individual's essence. Instead of rejecting the bold concepts frequently associated with imaginative insight, we should embrace the ethos of aspiration. This inspires individuals to reach for higher ideals, empowering them to chase their dreams no matter how unconventional they may seem to others.

Reflect on the methodology employed by the creators of the educational initiative TED. TED fosters the dissemination of transformative concepts, providing a stage for thought leaders across various disciplines to unveil their groundbreaking insights. This inclusive method ignites a shared spark of creativity, encouraging individuals to transcend traditional limits and chase their distinct aspirations.

Consider the concept of "Moonshot Thinking," as exemplified by Google, which inspires individuals to pursue ambitious and transformative objectives. This perspective encourages the exploration of transformative concepts, nurturing an environment rich in creativity and ambition. Through the endorsement of ambitious initiatives, Google fosters an inner drive among its employees, motivating them to pursue innovations that possess the potential to profoundly change the world.

Advocating for the principle of striving ignites a shared spark of creativity, not through conformity, but by fostering an environment of support that encourages individuals to share their distinct viewpoints. This holistic perspective, harnessing the shared potential of human creativity, fosters unexpected advancements and evolution. By fostering the exploration of creative vision, we access an immense well of potential, enabling individuals to make significant contributions to the progress of society.

5. The Power of Recognition: The Strive Principle

Empowering Self-Promotion: The "strive principle" is a profound motivation catalyst. When people are inspired to expand their horizons and are acknowledged for reaching their aspirations, they find the drive to succeed. This is exactly what those with profound insight do—consciously engage in actions that showcase their brilliance and worth. Nonetheless, the "strive principle" should not center solely on self-affirmation. Such accolades act as a powerful catalyst, inspiring individuals to explore innovative avenues for self-improvement and attain well-deserved acknowledgment, ultimately benefiting the greater community.

Reflect on the value of acknowledging meaningful achievements within entities such as Salesforce. Salesforce consistently honors the accomplishments of its employees through a range of recognition initiatives, including the esteemed "Top Performer" awards. Recognizing employees' contributions is a powerful catalyst, inspiring them to pursue excellence and nurturing an environment where continuous growth is encouraged and celebrated.

Consider the academic realm, where scholarships and awards acknowledge students' exceptional achievements. These honors recognize the dedication and catalyze other students to pursue comparable successes. Identifying excellence fosters a constructive cycle, inspiring individuals to expand their limits and significantly contribute to their domains.

The notion that an ostrich believes burying its head in the sand will eliminate danger is a poignant metaphor for employers who, in denial, overlook the profound impact of acknowledging meaningful achievements. This avoidance not only stifles growth but also perpetuates a cycle of unproductivity. Utilizing the strive principle can foster an atmosphere where individuals are recognized and inspired to reach their fullest potential. Through honoring accomplishments and fostering a culture of acknowledgment, communities, and institutions can unleash the complete capabilities of their individuals, propelling shared advancement and triumph.

Third Category: Institutional Influence and Societal Impact:

1. Cultivating Creativity: The Role of Government

Encouragement of Free Enterprise: Promoting free enterprise reflects a profound understanding that creativity is the cornerstone of progress in any thriving society. Consequently, these administrations implement measures that safeguard and promote entrepreneurial spirit and individual initiative. The rich soil of these environments nurtures the blossoming of imaginative ideas.

Reflect on the United States, where the Constitution distinctly safeguards free enterprise as an essential right. This safeguarding has fostered a setting that nurtures creativity and advancement. The essence of entrepreneurship, ignited by the liberty to embrace risks and delve into innovative concepts, has catalyzed remarkable technological progress and economic expansion.

Consider South Korea, where the government has taken proactive steps to foster innovation and entrepreneurship through strategic policies. Initiatives such as the "Creative Economy" program have offered essential funding and resources for startups, nurturing a dynamic tech ecosystem. The nurturing atmosphere present in South Korea has facilitated its emergence as a prominent force in technology and innovation on the global stage.

The advancement of contemporary technological societies is significantly attributed to governance structures that foster individual initiative and the spirit of free enterprise. By implementing policies that safeguard and cultivate creativity, authorities establish the essential environment for innovative concepts to thrive. This active engagement in fostering creativity guarantees ongoing growth and success.

1. Architects of Equality: Visionary Founders

Architects of Equality: The visionaries behind establishing remarkable nations transcended the role of mere politicians; they were essentially the architects of equality. Their imaginative insight reached its pinnacle in the profound understanding and foresight woven into the fabric of constitutions. These documents have endured through the ages, establishing a foundation rooted in equal rights for everyone, thus creating a timeless legacy of fairness and justice.

Reflect on the architects of the United States, whose aspirations materialized in formulating the U.S. Constitution. Influential figures such as Thomas Jefferson, James Madison, and Benjamin Franklin were instrumental in crafting a document embodying equality and individual rights. Their profound insight into human potential and unwavering dedication to fostering a just society culminated in creating a nation where every individual is afforded the chance to contribute and thrive.

Consider Nelson Mandela, a figure whose profound vision for a liberated and equitable South Africa catalyzed the end of apartheid and the formation of a democratic governance structure. Mandela's profound commitment to equality and visionary leadership was pivotal in shaping a new constitution that ensured equal rights and freedoms for every South African. His profound leadership reshaped a nation and ignited inspiration across the globe.

Their profound insight into human potential and visionary leadership established the groundwork for societies prioritizing equality and opportunity above all else. They emerged as profound creators of equality, leaving an indelible mark on the narrative of humanity. The visionaries behind great nations transcended the role of mere politicians; they were, in essence, architects of equality. Their imaginative insight manifested most profoundly in the foresight and understanding woven into the fabric of constitutions. These documents have endured through the ages, establishing a foundation rooted in the principle of equal rights for everyone, thus creating a timeless legacy of equity and justice.

Reflect on the founding fathers of the United States, whose aspirations led to the establishment of the U.S. Constitution. Influential figures such as Thomas Jefferson, James Madison, and Benjamin Franklin were instrumental in crafting a document embodying equality and individual rights. Their deep insight into human potential and unwavering dedication to fostering a just society culminated in creating a nation where everyone is empowered to contribute and thrive.

Consider Nelson Mandela's profound vision for a liberated and equitable South Africa, which catalyzed the dismantling of apartheid and paved the way for a democratic governance structure. Mandela's profound commitment to equality and visionary leadership were pivotal in shaping a new constitution that ensured equal rights and freedoms for every South African. His transformative vision reshaped a nation and ignited inspiration across the globe.

Their profound insight into human potential and visionary leadership established the groundwork for societies prioritizing equality and opportunity above all else. They emerged as profound creators of equality, leaving an indelible mark on humanity's narrative.

2. Acknowledging the Architects: Recognition of Visionaries

Recognizing Contributions: Individuals with a creative vision dedicate themselves to enhancing the human experience. Acknowledging their contributions openly rather than perceiving them solely as remuneration for their efforts is crucial. Individuals who imagine a more promising future merit acknowledgment for their dedication and perseverance in enhancing our shared reality. The genuine essence of a visionary's fulfillment lies in the deep transformation they evoke in the world rather than in the chase for monetary gains.

Reflect on the Nobel Prizes, a recognition bestowed upon those whose remarkable contributions have profoundly impacted humanity across domains like peace, literature, and science. These awards serve as a testament to the extraordinary accomplishments of individuals such as Malala Yousafzai, honored with the Nobel Peace Prize for her unwavering commitment to girls' education, and Albert Einstein, celebrated with the Nobel Prize in Physics for his revolutionary theories that transformed our understanding of the universe. This acknowledgment celebrates their contributions while motivating upcoming generations to strive for creativity and outstanding achievement.

Consider, for instance, the Presidential Medal of Freedom, which stands as the pinnacle of civilian recognition in the United States. Recipients encompass notable individuals such as Maya Angelou, whose profound literary and social contributions have indelibly shaped culture and society. Recognizing her contributions with this award acts as a profound encouragement for individuals to tap into their creative potential and pursue transformative endeavors.

Acknowledgment through accolades and heartfelt appreciation is a profound catalyst for inspiring the next wave of creative thinkers. In recognizing the wisdom of our elders and the insights of visionaries, we inspire individuals to harness their bravery and unleash their creativity, fostering a collective journey toward a transformative future. Honoring the accomplishments of those who envision the future cultivates an environment rich in gratitude and motivation, propelling ongoing advancement and creativity.

In what ways does this enhanced iteration resonate with your conceptualization of the book? Are you prepared to explore the next concept?

Fourth Category: Global Perspective and Knowledge Sharing:

1. Unlocking Potential: The Tapestry of Motive

The intricate tapestry of personal potential is woven from traits, aspirations, and self-imposed limitations, all of which interact to define the motivations that propel an individual onward. Those who seek deeper understanding recognize that these factors shape the core and breadth of an individual's motivation, ranging from fundamental safety to a condition of plenty.

Those who see beyond the ordinary understand the importance of addressing personal motivations. It is acknowledged that the drive stemming from within an individual surpasses the influence of any external incentives. An insightful leader can create a vision that sparks their inner passion by comprehending a person's strengths, weaknesses, and aspirations. For some individuals, this may signify the comfort of a home adorned with a picket fence; for others, it embodies the exhilarating pursuit of pushing boundaries to discover their true potential. By understanding each person's unique motivations, we can genuinely unlock their complete potential.

Reflect on the methodology employed by coaches and mentors as they customize their support to meet the unique needs of each athlete or mentee. For example, Phil Jackson, the iconic NBA coach, had a remarkable ability to grasp the distinct motivations driving each player. By attuning to their unique motivations and customizing his coaching techniques, Jackson was able to unlock the full potential of his team, guiding them to a series of championships.

Another illustration is how organizations such as Netflix cultivate an environment that embraces a variety of motivations. By cultivating a dynamic work atmosphere and fostering imaginative autonomy, Netflix empowers its employees to chase their passions and thrive in their positions. This tailored method of fostering motivation has significantly influenced the company's creativity and achievements.

These instances illustrate that customizing motivations is essential for realizing personal potential. Leaders who profoundly understand their followers' distinct motivations foster an atmosphere where each individual can flourish and play a vital role in advancing the group.

2. The Power of the Aspiring Dream: Constitutional Foundations

Inspiring High Aspirations: History reveals that the architects of remarkable nations were visionary individuals who understood the importance of establishing lofty and motivating goals for their people. Within their established frameworks, they integrated personal advantages that positioned individuals at the center of the pursuit of excellence.

The United States Constitution provides a quintessential illustration. The founding fathers profoundly understood the power of aspirational ideals. By establishing a framework that ensured equal rights and opportunities for all citizens, they cultivated a society where innovative ideas could thrive. This fundamental constitution serves as a beacon, motivating successive generations to pursue their aspirations and contribute to the collective welfare.

Reflect on the Preamble of the U.S. Constitution, which articulates the document's intent and establishes the noble aspirations of justice, tranquility, welfare, and liberty. The enduring principles have steered the nation through countless transformations and advancements over the centuries. The safeguards enshrined in the Constitution for free speech, the right to assemble, and other essential liberties have cultivated a landscape where innovation and creative expression can flourish.

Consider the Constitution of India, a document that embodies the ideals of equality, freedom, and justice and serves as a foundational framework for society. The architects of the Indian Constitution, guided by the visionary Dr. B.R. Ambedkar, sought to create a democratic society that empowers everyone to chase their dreams and ambitions. Focusing on social justice and equal opportunities has catalyzed remarkable progress in education, technology, and industry, playing a crucial role in shaping India's evolution as a dynamic democracy.

These examples demonstrate the profound influence of constitutional principles in fostering elevated ambitions. By integrating fundamental principles of equality and opportunity, innovative founders established structures that enabled individuals to pursue excellence and make meaningful contributions to the collective welfare. The enduring influence of these aspirational ideals persists, guiding nations and fostering progress for future generations.

3. **The Global Tapestry: Globalization and Knowledge Sharing**

Globalization of work and knowledge sharing are essential for harvesting the fruits of creative vision. As visionaries such as Henry Ford understood, true advancement emerges when individuals collaborate and exchange ideas beyond the confines of national borders. The intricate web of knowledge and skill fosters a rich exchange of ideas, paving the way for remarkable innovation.

Reflect on the emergence of the internet and its profound influence on the dissemination of knowledge across the globe. Platforms such as Wikipedia, GitHub, and LinkedIn serve as vital conduits for global connection, enabling individuals to exchange knowledge, collaborate on various projects, and cultivate professional relationships. These platforms are vital conduits for sharing thoughts and knowledge, fostering creativity and advancement in numerous domains. The open-source software movement exemplifies the power of collaboration, fostering the creation of resilient and widely adopted technologies through the shared efforts of developers worldwide.

Consider the profound implications of international collaboration in scientific research, exemplified by initiatives like the Human Genome Project. This remarkable pursuit united scholars from across the globe in the quest to chart the intricacies of the human genome. The collaborative exchange of knowledge and data within the project led to remarkable progress in the field of genetics, setting the stage for personalized medicine and various other significant medical innovations.

True creative vision transcends individual ownership; it yearns for collective expression. Integrating the distinct viewpoints of individuals into a cohesive framework fosters rapid, collective advancement. Envision a moment when brilliant minds from every corner of the world unite to confront the most profound challenges we face. This embodies the profound potential of globalization intertwined with the exchange of knowledge.

The interconnectedness of our world and the exchange of ideas foster an environment where innovation flourishes, enabling societies to reach unprecedented levels of achievement. Embracing the essence of the "strive principle," promoting acknowledgment, and nurturing worldwide cooperation allows us to tap into humanity's shared capabilities, propelling innovation and advancement.

Initiating Creative Vision: From Reflection to Action

Initiating creative vision is a journey that weaves together the threads of introspection, action, and empowerment. This process is a complex dance between reflecting on one's inner world and taking bold steps to bring visions to life. It's about unlocking the potential within, navigating the interplay between motivation and belief, and transforming ideas into reality. By embracing this multifaceted approach, we can tap into the wellspring of imagination and harness the power to shape our destinies. Let us delve into the intricate stages of initiating creative vision, exploring the diverse pathways that lead from reflection to action.

I. Awakening the Inner Vision:

1. The Unseen Seed: A Spark Ignites the Potential Within

The Dormant Seed. Deep within the intricate pathways of the human mind resides the essence of Creative Vision. This intrinsic Seed, present within every individual, quietly awaits the right impetus to awaken its potential and catalyze action. Unraveling the essence of this spark presents a profound enigma. What underlying motivations can break through the barriers of inactivity and release a surge of creativity?

The essence of creative vision is intricately tied to our fundamental yearning for new experiences and the expression of our true selves. When faced with a challenge or an innovative concept, our minds are stirred from their habitual patterns, fostering a space conducive to imaginative inquiry.

Reflect on the narrative of J.K. Rowling, who birthed the concept of Harry Potter amidst the stillness of a delayed train journey. This seemingly ordinary occurrence ignited a profound transformation within her, giving rise to a narrative that captivated the hearts and minds of countless individuals. The driving force behind her journey was a blend of her yearning to share narratives and her receptiveness to inspiration that arises in unforeseen instances.

Consider the case of Steve Jobs, who drew profound inspiration for the graphical user interface (GUI) from his experience at Xerox PARC. This meeting kindled a profound inspiration within him, ultimately culminating in creating the first Macintosh computer. Jobs' inquisitiveness and ambition to innovate technology ignited a creative vision that fundamentally altered the landscape of the tech industry.

The illustrations reveal how the latent seed of creative vision is ignited through a harmonious blend of internal drive and appropriate external influences. By cultivating our yearning for new experiences and authentic expression while staying receptive to inspiration, we can unlock the profound potential that resides within us.

2. The Whispering Pages: Unlocking the Secrets Within

The Transformative Influence of Literature on Thought and Understanding. Exploring diverse literature offers deep insights that are a significant impetus for igniting imaginative perspectives. These readings function as direct instructions and as subtle navigators, revealing the hidden gems that dwell within the psyche. We nurture the capacity to spark new ideas by intertwining existing knowledge in ways that question traditional perspectives, stimulating the imagination and bringing creativity to life from its dormant state.

The profound impact of engaging with insightful literature on the psyche is truly remarkable. These writings provoke our beliefs, revealing viewpoints that may be entirely unfamiliar to us. Deserting our mental comfort zone can ignite a surge of curious exploration as we endeavor to comprehend the unfamiliar and integrate it with our existing understanding of reality.

Reflect on the influence of engaging with works such as Joseph Campbell's "The Hero with a Thousand Faces." This exploration delves into the monomyth, often referred to as the hero's journey, a narrative framework that resonates through diverse cultures and eras. For numerous individuals, Campbell's revelations have opened fresh avenues for comprehending narrative and self-development, igniting inspiration in creators, directors, and intellectuals across the spectrum.

Another instance is Carl Jung's "The Red Book," a profoundly reflective and symbolic journey into the depths of the unconscious mind. Jung's work beckons individuals to delve into their inner landscapes, prompting a reevaluation of their perceptions and fostering a spirit of creative inquiry. For those who explore its depths, "The Red Book" serves as a subtle mentor, uncovering concealed dimensions of the mind and sparking innovative avenues of contemplation.

These examples demonstrate how the subtle yet profound messages found within insightful readings can act as catalysts for awakening one's creative vision. Through the act of questioning our beliefs and broadening our viewpoints, they awaken a profound energy within us, fostering a wave of transformative creativity and innovation.

3. The Shifted Lens: The World Transformed by Inner Vision

The Town Transformed[10] explores a captivating dimension of human existence: our inner vision significantly shapes our perception of the surrounding world. When the flame of creativity awakens within us, the fabric of reality transforms in remarkable ways. The commonplace elements of our everyday existence often hold the power to metamorphose into the remarkable, uncovering the extraordinary possibilities beneath the surface of the ordinary. This is not just a mental illusion; it uncovers the dynamic landscape within us.

Reflect on the profound impact of J.R.R. Tolkien's passion for languages and ancient myths in shaping his imaginative universe. A seemingly straightforward bedtime tale for his children blossomed into Middle-earth's intricate and profound realm. His inner perspective transformed his understanding of narrative and shaped the minds of countless readers and creators, elevating mundane settings into the extraordinary worlds of "The Lord of the Rings."

---

[10] As enrichment regarding "The Twon Transformed," this concept is related to the concept of transformative perception and mindset shifts. These ideas are explored in various psychological and philosophical texts, which align well with your theme of inner vision shaping our perception of the world.

- **Transformative Perception:** This concept is discussed in works by Carl Jung and William James, who explore how our inner vision and creativity can alter our experience of reality. Jung's ideas on the collective unconscious and archetypes and James's thoughts on the stream of consciousness both highlight how internal perspectives can transform our external reality.
- **Mindset Shifts:** The notion of changing one's mindset to alter perception is well-documented in psychology. Carol Dweck's research on fixed and growth mindsets1 and Jacob Towery's work on the power of changing mindsets1 provide a solid foundation for understanding how our inner vision can reshape our perception of the world.
- **Psychogeography:** This field, particularly the works of Guy Debord and Iain Sinclair, examines how urban environments influence our psychological experiences and behaviors. It aligns with your idea of transforming the mundane into the remarkable through inner vision.

Frida Kahlo's unique journey illustrates how her personal experiences and emotions reshaped her understanding of reality. Her vibrant and dreamlike artworks, intricately connected to her inner perception, portray a realm filled with profound hues and meaning. Kahlo's remarkable capacity to harness her suffering and enthusiasm through her artistry enabled her to elevate the mundane into profound representations of self and heritage.

We start to perceive the world anew, attuned to nuances and interconnections that previously eluded our awareness. This heightened awareness nurtures our artistic pursuit to convey the beauty and intricacy of a previously unobserved reality surrounding us. These instances demonstrate that a change in our inner perspective can profoundly alter not just our understanding but also the reality we manifest.

4. The Architect Within Charting the Course to Creation

Major Purpose Birthed. Establishing a clear primary purpose is the essential groundwork and guiding force for transforming concepts into tangible actions. This serves as a foundational framework for our creative exploration, steering us toward formulating a strategic approach to achieve our envisioned goals.

A sense of purpose instills a profound motivation within the mind. It provides us the motivation and resilience to confront challenges and continue our journey toward realizing our creative aspirations. The notion that our endeavors serve a greater purpose ignites our enthusiasm and sustains us through challenging moments and bleak days.

Reflect on the case of Thomas Edison, whose fundamental aim was to illuminate the world with electric light. Edison's steadfast dedication to this objective propelled him through countless unsuccessful trials. His profound sense of purpose instilled in him remarkable resilience, enabling him to persist through challenges. This ultimately led to the groundbreaking invention of the electric lightbulb, a transformative force in modern existence.

Consider Malala Yousafzai, a figure whose mission centers on championing girls' education worldwide. In the face of formidable challenges that could easily deter many, Malala's unwavering commitment to her mission propels her forward in her advocacy efforts. Her profound sense of purpose fueled her endeavors and motivated countless individuals globally to champion educational equality.

These instances demonstrate that possessing a distinct, central purpose acts as an inner guide, steering innovators through obstacles and aiding them in realizing their aspirations. By exploring and accepting their purpose, individuals cultivate the motivation essential for creating a meaningful legacy.

5. The Guiding Star: Intrinsic Motivation

A Clear Intention. Motivation transforms into an influential beacon of direction when one possesses a well-articulated sense of purpose. Driven by a profound sense of purpose and a clear intention, this inner surge of motivation embodies a genuine aspiration to bring forth the creations that reside within us. It is an inner drive that propels us forward in the face of challenges and setbacks.

The flickering flame of intrinsic motivation catalyzes creativity and vision, illuminating the path forward. This profound energy propels us past the ordinary, offering a sense of completion in the uncharted territories of our minds. The inner compass we possess guides us toward the challenges that ignite our passion and vitality, embarking us on a profound journey of self-exploration.

Reflect on the narrative of Vincent van Gogh, whose deep-seated motivation propelled him to create in the face of profound personal challenges. Van Gogh's genuine dedication to art and the pursuit of self-expression served as his beacon, driving him to create more than 2,000 pieces in merely ten years. His motivation stemmed not from external accolades but from a profound, intrinsic yearning to encapsulate the beauty he observed in the world.

Consider the remarkable journey of Marie Curie, driven by an innate desire to comprehend radioactivity, which led her to make transformative discoveries. In the face of countless challenges, such as scarce resources and societal constraints, Curie's steadfast dedication to her scientific mission propelled her to become the first woman to receive a Nobel Prize and the sole individual to achieve Nobel Prizes in two distinct scientific disciplines. Her inner drive served as a beacon, illuminating the journey toward her extraordinary accomplishments.

These instances illustrate the profound impact of intrinsic motivation, propelling visionaries to transcend their boundaries. By attuning to this inner guidance, individuals adeptly maneuver through obstacles with grit, leading to remarkable achievements. The essence of intrinsic motivation illuminates the path of creative exploration, fostering a profound journey toward self-awareness and personal fulfillment.

6. The Unveiled Path: Clarity of Vision

The Unveiled Path: As we bring a lucid vision into focus, the entire landscape of our existence transforms before our eyes.

Our vision sharpens, allowing us to recognize possibilities that may have previously eluded our awareness. This occurrence is known as the revealed journey. We begin to reflect on why these opportunities eluded our awareness in the past. This fresh perspective ignites our passion, driving us onward with a revitalized sense of purpose.

Reflect on the profound impact that a clear vision had on Albert Einstein's life. Before his revolutionary theories, Einstein endured a prolonged period that appeared to be a professional standstill. Yet, as the clarity of his vision for the theory of relativity sharpened, the once-ordinary elements of his work evolved into a dynamic realm of potential. This newfound understanding empowered him to make crucial choices and focus his energies, resulting in groundbreaking progress in the field of physics.

Consider the journey of Oprah Winfrey, whose distinct vision for fostering authentic storytelling and empowerment reshaped her career and the entire media landscape. Winfrey's profound sense of direction illuminated pathways to engage with audiences on a deeper level. This newfound clarity ignited her passion and steered her toward making thoughtful decisions that broadened her reach and significance.

As one embarks on the journey of creative expression, a newfound clarity begins to illuminate the vision. The once obscure haze of ambiguity gradually dissipates, revealing a vibrant expanse brimming with potential and opportunity. This understanding empowers us to navigate our choices, establish our values, and face obstacles in our journey. By embracing the revealed journey, we tap into the energy and concentration essential for manifesting our creative aspirations.

II. Building Confidence and Belief:

1. Silencing the Inner Critic: The Rise of Confidence

Unwavering Belief. Self-doubt stands as a formidable adversary to the clarity and brilliance of creative vision. In awakening the creative vision, we cultivate a sense of self-assurance. When we align with our true purpose and establish a clear plan, the shadows of fear and doubt begin to dissipate, empowering us to confidently manifest our ideas into the world.

The path to artistic awakening is often fraught with the weight of self-doubt, making it a challenging endeavor. The inner critic, fueled by societal pressures and previous missteps, often seeks to dampen the sparks of our aspirations. By confronting these restrictive beliefs and nurturing self-compassion, a sense of quiet confidence emerges. We begin to embrace our intuition, recognizing that the journey of creativity is frequently chaotic.

Reflect on the path of Maya Angelou, whose formative years were shaped by adversity and uncertainty within herself. In the face of adversity, Angelou discovered her authentic expression through the art of writing and poetry. She transmuted her suffering into impactful literary expressions by facing her inner critic and fully accepting her creative vision. Her unwavering belief and growing self-assurance not only quieted her uncertainties but also motivated countless individuals across the globe.

Consider the narrative of Vincent van Gogh, a figure who grappled with profound mental health challenges and pervasive self-doubt during his existence. His unwavering commitment to his artistic vision enabled him to produce masterpieces that still echo in the present day. Van Gogh's capacity to quiet his inner doubts and embrace his artistic journey in the face of societal pressures and personal challenges illustrates the emergence of self-assurance through unwavering belief.

These examples demonstrate that we can cultivate the confidence essential for pursuing our creative aspirations by quieting the inner critic and nurturing self-compassion. Embracing our intuition and the inherent chaos of the journey empowers us to manifest our ideas into reality with steadfast resolve.

2. The Architect's Trust: The Power of Belief

The Sound Plan fosters a profound sense of conviction within us. The intrinsic confidence in our approach cultivates a space conducive to an elevated creative viewpoint. We embody a sense of confidence and find inspiration to act from the awareness that a clearly articulated strategic framework is in place. This belief acts as a cognitive structure in the face of our inevitable challenges. Our ability to face challenges is strengthened when we trust in the structure we have created.

Belief serves as the foundation for the architect—the essential element upon which the structure of creative vision is constructed. Without a profound conviction in our ability to transform our ideas into reality, our vision remains merely a fleeting dream. Individuals with vision can turn abstract concepts into concrete outcomes by fostering self-belief and recognizing their capacity for innovation.

Reflect on the case of Walt Disney, whose conviction in the enchantment of narrative and animation propelled him to establish the Disney empire. In the face of countless obstacles, Disney's steadfast belief in his vision propelled him forward, enabling him to create a realm of enchantment that continues to mesmerize audiences. The foundation of his achievements lay in his unwavering faith in the transformative potential of imagination and creativity.

Another example is Steve Jobs, who held a profound conviction in the transformative potential of technology. Jobs' unwavering belief in his vision for Apple products, despite encountering doubt and challenges, propelled him to pursue innovation with relentless determination. This unwavering conviction empowered him to develop innovations that transformed the technology landscape and influenced contemporary existence.

The examples illustrate that the architect's trust—the essence of belief—is crucial for manifesting creative visions into reality. By cultivating a deep conviction in their concepts and capacity for innovation, those with a visionary mindset establish a solid groundwork that allows their aspirations to manifest.

3. The Ripple Effect: The Power of Shared Vision

The Window of Joy suggests that creativity thrives on connection—on the act of sharing our visions with those we cherish, who amplify our efforts, elevate our dedication, and provide essential positive reinforcement. The presence of excitement and encouragement reflected in others' eyes fosters within us a deeper conviction that our aspirations are indeed attainable. This uplifting cycle enhances people's drive, prompting them to explore and develop innovative solutions.

Reflect on the narrative of the Wright brothers, Orville and Wilbur, whose collective aspiration for powered flight was strengthened by their unwavering support and encouragement for one another. Their joint endeavors and mutual passion fostered a constructive cycle that enabled them to accomplish the inaugural successful flight of an airplane. This ripple effect transcended their collaboration, igniting a belief in the potential of aviation and challenging the limits of human flight.

Consider the partnership between John Lennon and Paul McCartney of The Beatles. Their collective aspiration for groundbreaking music and their capacity to motivate one another resulted in the birth of enduring melodies that persist in shaping artists across the globe. The mutual inspiration and support they discovered within their creative journey ignited a transformative wave, breathing life into their innovative concepts and redefining the music landscape.

Inspiration flows from one mind to another, igniting a spark of innovation and imagination. In our discussions, we share our insights with certainty, inviting others to join in the journey of understanding. This ripple effect ignites a spark for those who may find themselves in the shadowy realms of self-doubt. Through exchanging thoughts, tools, and support, we cultivate a reality that surpasses our original expectations—a shared conviction in the transformative potential of creativity.

4. The Long Game: A Vision Beyond the Horizon

The Vision Horizon: An awakened creative vision transcends the pursuit of immediate satisfaction. Rather, it promotes nurturing with an outlook focused on the long haul. Genuine creative satisfaction emerges from endeavors that leave a profound and enduring mark. Concentrating on the broader vision empowers us to make choices that align with a more significant purpose, striving for something beyond our individual selves. This transformation in our mindset allows us to discover significance and intention in the act of creation, even when the benefits are not immediately apparent.

Genuine creative insight unfolds over time, requiring endurance rather than haste. It revolves around a profound dedication and the ability to navigate challenges, unpredictability, and setbacks. We cultivate the strength to maneuver through uncertainty by embracing this broader perspective. We cultivate an appreciation for the journey itself, embracing the complexities and nuances of creative exploration just as much as the fulfillment that the outcome may offer.

Reflect on the path of Maya Angelou, whose enduring dedication to writing, activism, and the arts has profoundly influenced both literature and the pursuit of social justice. Her work encompasses many years, demonstrating a commitment to enduring influence over fleeting recognition. Angelou's perspective transcended her era, shaping the thoughts and actions of innumerable people and causes through her profound expressions and steadfast dedication to equity.

Consider the contributions of Jonas Salk, the visionary behind the polio vaccine. Salk's enduring aspiration extended beyond merely discovering a cure; it was to eliminate a profoundly destructive illness. His unwavering commitment to this objective demanded years of inquiry, resilience, and a profound consideration for the collective well-being. Salk made a notable decision to forgo patenting the vaccine, placing the well-being of humanity above individual gain. His foresight and unwavering dedication have preserved countless lives and persist in motivating advancements in medicine.

These examples demonstrate that authentic creative vision demands an unwavering gaze toward the horizon and a commitment to enduring aspirations. Embracing this perspective allows us to discover purpose and fulfillment in our journey as we navigate challenges with resilience and strive to create a meaningful impact.

5. The Unmasking: The Power of Self-Questioning

The awakened creative vision embraces self-inquiry as a powerful instrument for revealing one's true potential. This introspective examination compels individuals to step beyond their comfort zones by challenging restrictive beliefs. Through introspection and inquiry, we uncover that the root of our dissatisfaction with the current state of affairs nudges us toward higher ambitions.

Self-reflection serves as a profound mechanism that reveals the depths of our creative capabilities. Through the relentless pursuit of inquiry and the courage to confront established norms, we liberate ourselves from the confines of familiarity, paving the way for fresh opportunities. This process of self-examination acts as a tool, carving away the hardened layers of uncertainty to reveal the creator within, ready to shape our aspirations into reality.

a) **Why accept minor gains when greater opportunities lie ahead?** This inquiry invites us to acknowledge the unconscious boundaries we impose on ourselves. It establishes elevated standards and inspires us to strive for a more fulfilling and meaningful existence.

b) **What inner voice compels me to pursue greater aspirations?** This inquiry invites us to delve deep within ourselves and attune to the creative desires that might have been stifled. We uncover profound passions within ourselves and release a surge of creative vitality.

c) **Why settle for less when the universe calls you to greatness?** This inquiry invites us to envision grand possibilities, serving as a reminder that with self-belief, we can accomplish remarkable feats. Embracing bold aspirations enables us to transcend our familiar boundaries and access the depths of our creative capabilities.

Reflect on the path of Frida Kahlo, who engaged in deep self-inquiry to transmute her suffering and challenges into remarkable artistic expressions. Kahlo's reflective journey enabled her to reveal profound feelings and convey them through her art, which still connects with viewers across the globe.

Consider the narrative of Howard Schultz, the former CEO of Starbucks, who engaged in profound self-reflection regarding his aspirations for the company. Schultz's deep reflection and courage to question conventional norms resulted in groundbreaking business strategies and a significant transformation within the coffee sector.

These examples demonstrate that self-reflection is essential for tapping into one's creative capabilities. We uncover our authentic capabilities through self-reflection and questioning restrictive thoughts, creating a pathway for profound creativity.

III. Translating Vision into Action:

1. The Alchemist's Fire: Transmuting Belief into Action

Beyond Contemplation highlights the importance of engaging in active meditation. Belief devoid of action is lifeless. Once we have ignited our creative vision through self-inquiry, it is essential to transform our beliefs into tangible actions. This is the moment when transformation begins to unfold. We tap into this unique energy within ourselves and bring our vision to life through tangible actions.

This shift from reflection to execution holds significant importance in understanding human behavior. One must delve deeper into these concepts. As we embark on our journey of growth and cultivate the confidence needed to confront the challenges that lie ahead, our aspirations begin to materialize, fueled by the transformative power of our actions. A creative vision remains a fleeting notion, lacking substance until we actively engage in the process of manifesting it into reality. It encourages taking action rather than remaining passive in the face of uncertainty. Integrating our deepest beliefs into our daily existence infuses our aspirations with vitality through each choice.

Reflect on the narrative surrounding Steve Jobs and the inception of the original Macintosh computer. Jobs' vision for a personal computer featuring a graphical user interface was revolutionary, yet it demanded more than mere conviction. He diligently chased this vision, gathering a team, refining the technology, and overcoming various obstacles. The outcome was a groundbreaking innovation that reshaped the technology landscape. The transformative force that manifested his vision was the capacity to transform conviction into tangible steps.

Consider Elon Musk's endeavors; his initiatives, such as SpaceX and Tesla, originated from bold aspirations. Musk's dedication to these aspirations necessitated audacious steps, ranging from obtaining financial backing to overcoming technical challenges. His commitment to embodying his convictions has catalyzed remarkable progress in space exploration and sustainable energy, transforming once-elusive aspirations into tangible achievements.

These instances illustrate that transforming belief into action is crucial for manifesting creative aspirations. We manifest our aspirations into concrete realities through intentional actions and steadfast resilience in the face of obstacles. The transformative power of action serves as the essential force that brings our aspirations into reality.

2. Seizing the Moment: The Power of Action

The Prospect's Opportunity conveys the essential wisdom of embracing the present and acting decisively without hesitation. Imaginative insight carries minimal significance if one is not willing to seize the possibilities it offers. Procrastination presents a formidable obstacle to the flow of creativity. Taking prompt action reflects our commitment to our vision and opens doors to possibilities that might not have existed otherwise.

Imaginative insight thrives when paired with purposeful execution. Delaying action erodes ambitions, and uncertainty fosters stagnation. By embracing the chance to respond promptly, we sustain and amplify the energy sparked by those early endeavors. This confident perspective fosters a belief in our abilities and drives us to pursue creative satisfaction.

Reflect on Jeff Bezos's narrative and the inception of Amazon. Bezos discerned the vast possibilities within the nascent internet landscape and took decisive action to establish an online bookstore. His ability to make firm decisions and embrace opportunities propelled Amazon's swift growth, transforming it into a worldwide e-commerce powerhouse. Bezos' capacity to swiftly implement his vision revolutionized not just his enterprise but also the entire retail landscape.

Consider the narrative of J.K. Rowling, who embraced the opportunity that arose when she envisioned the concept for

Harry Potter during an unexpected train journey delay.[11] Rather than allowing the notion to dissipate, she promptly engaged with it by articulating her reflections and crafting the narrative. Her swift response and unwavering commitment to her vision culminated in creating one of the most successful literary franchises ever known.

These examples demonstrate that the essence of action resides in its capacity to transform imaginative ideas into tangible outcomes. By taking bold actions and welcoming opportunities as they present themselves, we move closer to creative satisfaction and unlock new paths to achievement.

3. Effortless Efficacy: The Flow State

Envision a situation where your creative vision transports you into a seamless state of productivity, liberated from any tension. When in a state of flow, an individual optimally harnesses their mental and emotional capacities to accomplish a task, leading to peak efficiency and effectiveness. Minimal exertion appears needed, and time effortlessly slips away. When we enter a flow state, our creativity and productivity reach new heights.

The explanation for these phenomena lies in the psychological understanding that creative vision directs our focus and inspires motivation. When a profound vision guides one, one can transcend distractions, harnessing one's focus to direct one's energies with greater efficacy.

---

[11] During a delayed train ride from Manchester to London, J.K. Rowling had the idea for the Harry Potter series. She spent the entire four-hour drive brainstorming the book's ideas because she didn't have a pen and was too embarrassed to ask for one. It's amazing how a seemingly ordinary circumstance, like a train delay, can give rise to such a magical universe.
https://stories.jkrowling.com/en-us/harrypotter/the-magical-journey/

Reflect on the journey of athletes as they reach their pinnacle of performance. In a flow state, individuals feel "in the zone," where their actions unfold effortlessly, and everything harmonizes seamlessly. This elevated level of concentration and ease enables individuals to excel, appearing to do so effortlessly.

Another example is the journey of artistic creation. Artists such as Jackson Pollock experienced profound immersion while creating his drip paintings. Pollock articulated his approach as entering a nearly trance-like state, where he experienced a profound connection with his canvas, enabling his creativity to emerge fluidly and spontaneously. This profound engagement led to transformative creations that reshaped the landscape of abstract expressionism.

In essence, 'Flow' represents that profound mental state we enter when fully immersed in the creative process of creating something new. Throughout this journey, the concepts of time and identity fade away. All experiences seem seamless, and challenges reveal themselves as chances for personal development. We unlock the potential for our most innovative and impactful endeavors in this state.

4. The Reflective Path: Learning from the Journey

The arrival of that pivotal moment when self-reflection intensifies compels us to delve deeply into our own consciousness. Exploring our memory processes can reveal profound insights into our creative potential. This introspective journey reveals our constraints, steering us toward future development. It allows us to recognize our development and find pleasure in our achievements.

Self-reflection serves as a powerful catalyst for personal development and understanding. By thoughtfully analyzing our experiences, we can uncover recurring behaviors and develop approaches to enhance our creative pursuits. Through contemplation of our successes and failures, we glean important lessons that aid us in deciphering the complexities of our creative journey. We cultivate the ability to identify patterns, embrace and honor achievements, and reflect on setbacks as integral components of our journey toward mastery.

Reflect on journaling, frequently embraced by those with the foresight to capture their insights, journeys, and development. Leonardo da Vinci's notebooks exemplify this practice beautifully. His intricate sketches, keen observations, and thoughtful reflections showcased his brilliance and laid out a pathway for his artistic exploration. Through persistent contemplation of his endeavors, da Vinci uncovered profound insights that propelled his groundbreaking contributions to art, science, and engineering.

Another illustration is the iterative journey embraced by accomplished entrepreneurs like Sara Blakely, the visionary behind Spanx. Blakely's practice of introspection regarding her business choices, deriving insights from her missteps, and acknowledging minor achievements have been fundamental to her success. Her openness to introspection enabled her to confront obstacles and consistently enhance her offerings and approaches.

The examples presented underscore the vital role of introspection in creative development. Through self-reflection, we cultivate a richer awareness of our creative potential, draw insights from our experiences, and lay the groundwork for ongoing growth and innovation.

5.   The Architect of Destiny: The Power of Conviction

The journey of transforming thoughts allows creative vision to transcend mere imagination, becoming a powerful instrument of destiny. Like a transformative tool, it enables us to reshape our thoughts, beliefs, and attitudes into the foundation of the life we aspire to create. We can achieve an endless journey by fully embracing our vision's strength and transforming our narratives. It is fascinating to consider that within each individual lies an untapped reservoir of strength, patiently awaiting revelation.

Reflect on the path of Oprah Winfrey, who transformed her difficult upbringing into a remarkable ascent as a worldwide media powerhouse and generous benefactor. Winfrey's steadfast belief in her narrative and mission to uplift others enabled her to reshape her existence and impact countless lives. Through the power of her mindset, convictions, and perspectives, she constructed a legacy that satisfied her dreams and established a space for many others to unlock their true capabilities.

Consider Elon Musk's unwavering belief in his vision for space exploration and sustainable energy, which has propelled him to establish innovative companies such as SpaceX and Tesla. Musk's capacity to transform his ideas and convictions into tangible outcomes through unwavering effort and creativity has revolutionized sectors and unveiled new horizons for humanity. His transformative thinking has converted lofty aspirations into concrete successes, motivating others to chase their innovative ambitions.

These examples demonstrate that the strength of belief is essential for turning imaginative ideas into tangible outcomes. By delving into the power of our vision and transforming our narratives, we reveal the hidden potential that resides within us. This transformative process empowers us to mold our future and construct the life we envision, driven by a steadfast conviction in our capacity to create and innovate.

IV. Embracing Imagination and Freedom:

1. The Limitless Currency: The Power of Imagination

The Beautiful Discovery: The power of creative vision bestows upon us an endlessly precious resource—the currency of imagination. In contrast to material wealth, which can fade or lose value in challenging times, this spiritual abundance remains unblemished and enduring. This represents an ongoing reservoir of boundless abilities and strengths that nourish our creativity throughout our lives. This revelation uncovers a deep reality: our most valuable asset is not found outside ourselves but resides in the limitless potential of our thoughts. This is referred to as a "beautiful discovery" as it unveils a wellspring of abundance that belongs to us forever.

Reflect on Walt Disney's enduring impact. His creativity crafted a realm of magic that still captivates countless generations. Disney's boundless creativity has given rise to characters, narratives, and experiences that resonate across generations. His imaginative vision, driven by an endless source of creativity, forged a realm of happiness and originality that continues to resonate today.

Consider the insights of the theoretical physicist Albert Einstein, who profoundly stated, "Imagination is more important than knowledge." Knowledge may be confined, yet imagination encompasses the vastness of existence, fostering advancement and igniting transformation. Einstein's revolutionary theories in physics emerged from his capacity to envision possibilities that transcended the traditional limits of scientific thought. His visionary perspective reshaped our comprehension of the cosmos and persisted in motivating the pursuit of scientific inquiry.

These examples demonstrate that the strength of imagination is a priceless resource, driving us toward innovative exploration and advancement. By embracing this boundless currency, we connect with an infinite wellspring of creativity and insight, enhancing our existence and environment.

2. Shattering the Chains: Freedom from False Commitments

The Unrestrained Self: A creative vision serves as a profound catalyst, empowering individuals to break free from the constraints of misguided obligations. This invites introspection, revealing the essence of our strength and genuineness while encouraging us to examine every facet of our identity. As we embark on the journey to achieve our aspirations, we swiftly recognize and deconstruct the constraining beliefs and external pressures that have dictated our actions. This transformative journey liberates us from the self-imposed constraints we often create, urging us to pursue the authentic desires of our hearts.

Reflect on the narrative of Henry David Thoreau, who withdrew to Walden Pond to embrace simplicity and rediscover his authentic self. Thoreau's choice to liberate himself from societal norms enabled him to delve into his creative vision and philosophical concepts unencumbered. His experience at Walden gave rise to "Walden," a piece that remains a source of inspiration for individuals striving for authenticity and simplicity.

Consider the journey of Maya Angelou, a life defined by transformative experiences that enabled her to transcend societal and personal limitations. Angelou discovered her true voice through her writing and activism and harnessed it to motivate others to embrace their own. Her memoir, "I Know Why the Caged Bird Sings," profoundly explores her path toward self-realization and freedom from misleading obligations.

The concept of genius freedom reflects a profound expression of the authentic creativity that resides within every individual. By embracing our creative vision and liberating ourselves from constraining beliefs, we unveil our authentic potential and heed the call of our hearts. This personal exploration and freedom path empowers us to embrace our true selves and express our creativity without limitations.

3. The Unrecognized Seed: The Peril of Apathy

Constraints of Unawareness: Many individuals remain oblivious to their creative potential, confined by self-imposed limitations born from ignorance and indifference. These unseen barriers significantly hinder the ability to express creativity. An individual may possess a deep desire to paint, yet self-esteem issues or the fear of failure can inhibit that expression. Such concealed obstacles confine an individual within the constraints of their true potential. Conquering your "bars of ignorance" is essential for unleashing the creativity that resides within you.

Reflect on the path of Harper Lee, who possessed a profound narrative within her yet faced initial reluctance to embrace writing, hindered by self-doubt and the weight of societal expectations. Through her friends' unwavering encouragement and support, she transcended her fears and crafted "To Kill a Mockingbird," a novel that emerged as a literary masterpiece. By transcending her limitations of understanding, Lee liberated her imaginative capabilities and left an enduring mark on the realm of literature.

Consider the case of Vincent van Gogh, a figure who grappled with profound mental health challenges and pervasive self-doubt. In the face of internal struggles, van Gogh's unwavering passion for painting propelled him to produce some of the most renowned masterpieces in art history. His path to overcoming his limitations in the face of adversity enabled him to unlock his creative potential.

These examples demonstrate that recognizing and transcending internal obstacles is essential for unleashing creativity. By facing our fears and self-doubt, we can liberate ourselves from the constraints that hinder us and fully embrace our authentic creative potential.

4. Empowerment Through Ownership: Taking Charge

The Turning Point: Embracing an entrepreneurial spirit transcends mere passion; it beckons you to elevate your identity from an employee to an owner. Through a shift in mindset, one can reframe appropriate roles and endeavors from mere external obligations into fulfilling personal journeys. When we take control of our existence, we tap into a wellspring of intrinsic motivation that leads us to the fulfillment of our creative aspirations. This represents a profound transformation in how we approach decision-making.

Reflect on the case of Howard Schultz, the former leader of Starbucks. Schultz's evolution from working at a coffee equipment company to becoming the owner of Starbucks exemplifies this remarkable transformation. Through a deep commitment to his vision of crafting a distinctive coffeehouse experience, Schultz redefined Starbucks, elevating it to a global phenomenon. His unique perspective enabled him to identify possibilities in situations others perceived as constraints, propelling the company's advancement and creativity.

Consider the narrative of Steve Jobs, who embraced his creative vision and transformed Apple into a formidable technological force. Jobs' capacity to transition from an employee mindset to that of an owner allowed him to embrace bold decisions and undertake risks that transformed the tech landscape. His dedication to taking charge and overseeing his endeavors enabled him to manifest his innovative concepts, influencing the trajectory of technology.

These instances illustrate that taking ownership is essential for unleashing creative potential. By cultivating an entrepreneurial mindset and asserting control over our lives, we unlock a profound inner motivation that guides us toward creative fulfillment and achievement. This shift in mindset enables us to transform our external responsibilities into deeply personal passions, resulting in meaningful and fulfilling pursuits.

5. The Power of Now: From Thought to Action

The Power of Now: Immediate action ignites the spark of creative vision. Intelligent thought serves as the initial response to the invitation for planning and strategizing, marking just the commencement of a deeper exploration. What truly matters is the pressing need for action, the unwavering drive to transform our concepts into tangible realities. This empowers us to transition from being passive recipients of life's circumstances to becoming engaged architects of our futures. The passage highlights the significance of embracing the present, stressing the importance of making tangible progress toward our aspirations in the here and now.

Reflect on the journey of Richard Branson, who embraced the opportunity to launch his inaugural business endeavor, a student magazine, during his teenage years. Branson's bold choices and readiness to act swiftly in pursuit of his vision established the groundwork for the Virgin Group, a worldwide conglomerate spanning multiple sectors. His capacity to translate his thoughts into action and fully engage with the present moment has propelled his achievements in entrepreneurship.

Consider the journey of Marie Curie, whose pioneering research in radioactivity was sparked by her choice to explore the enigmatic element radium. Curie's swift response and unwavering commitment to her scientific ideals resulted in the groundbreaking discovery of polonium and radium, which earned her two Nobel Prizes and transformed the landscape of medicine. Her unwavering dedication to decisive action turned her aspirations into remarkable accomplishments.

These examples demonstrate that the essence of the present moment is found in our capacity to take decisive action and welcome opportunities as they arise. We transition from passive observers to engaged contributors in crafting our futures by taking deliberate actions toward our vision. The essence of the present moment drives our journey, transforming our reflections into concrete experiences.

V. Leveraging Vision for Collective Progress:

1. The Creative Exchange: Leveraging Your Vision

Exchange for Creative Works: Many individuals face the daunting challenge of financial limitations when striving to convey their creative visions. Yet, the essence of creative vision offers artists a profound response: the dynamic of creative interchange. Our thoughts frequently transcend the boundaries imposed by financial constraints. Presenting our concepts to others enhances our likelihood of drawing in investors and collaborators willing to support our initiatives in return for a portion of the earnings. This underscores the importance of transparent communication and collaboration in fostering creativity.

Reflect on the journey of J.K. Rowling, who faced significant challenges in securing a publisher for her Harry Potter series. Despite countless rejections, she remained steadfast in presenting her vision, ultimately achieving a publishing deal. This collaboration eased her financial burdens and offered the encouragement necessary to manifest her creative aspirations. Rowling's journey highlights the profound impact of harnessing imaginative collaboration to navigate challenges.

Consider the emergence of crowdfunding platforms such as Kickstarter, where innovators present their ideas to a worldwide audience. Initiatives like the Oculus Rift, a virtual reality headset, attracted considerable interest and financial support via Kickstarter. By articulating their vision to prospective supporters, the creators successfully garnered the essential resources and backing to bring their groundbreaking product to fruition. Marketing an inactive creative vision has emerged as a prevalent and impactful method for funding artistic pursuits.

These instances illustrate how harnessing imaginative perspectives via open conversation and teamwork can reveal fresh possibilities and assets. Through meaningful interactions and exchanging our thoughts, we can turn financial limitations into opportunities for development and achievement.

2. The Serendipity Magnet: Attracting Opportunity

The Human Magnet: A creative vision is a powerful force that attracts positive opportunities into our lives. It also serves as a beacon for unexpected occurrences; opportunities gravitate toward us like moths drawn to light. When we engage with intention and awareness, our vision generates a ripple effect by activating such an energetic field. As we immerse ourselves in realizing our vision, we subtly communicate our purpose to the universe, drawing in the necessary resources and connections to transform our ideas into tangible existence.

Reflect on the path of Alexander Fleming, whose serendipitous finding of penicillin transformed the landscape of medicine. Fleming's keen awareness and initiative in laboratory endeavors culminated in this unexpected discovery. His innovative perspective in bacteriology attracted the chance to uncover the first antibiotic, a breakthrough that has preserved innumerable lives.

Consider, for instance, the innovative invention of Velcro by George de Mestral. During a hunting excursion, de Mestral observed burrs adhering to his garments and his dog's coat. His inquisitive nature and active engagement with this phenomenon culminated in the creation of Velcro. De Mestral's innovative insight opened the door to this opportunity, turning a basic observation into a commonly utilized fastening system.

These examples demonstrate how a creative vision serves as a powerful force, drawing in unexpected opportunities. We communicate our desires to the cosmos through mindfulness and initiative, attracting the tools and connections essential for manifesting our visions. This phenomenon of attracting fortunate coincidences amplifies our capacity to transform imaginative ideas into tangible outcomes.

3. The Look-and-Key Principle: Unlocking Potential

Beyond Closed Doors: The "look-and-key principle" implies that creative vision functions as a key, unlocking doors to new possibilities and facilitating exploration in uncharted territories. Viewing the world through a lens of creativity and potential transforms mundane experiences into avenues for groundbreaking ideas.

Much like a key unlocking a door, our creative vision enables us to recognize and embrace new opportunities that come our way. It empowers us to imagine opportunities where others perceive constraints and inspires us to take action on our thoughts. Recognizing the essence of potential holds equal significance to our steps to manifest our aspirations. By grasping and implementing the "look-and-key principle," we empower ourselves to transcend traditional limits and achieve remarkable outcomes.

Reflect on Steve Jobs's narrative. He recognized the possibilities of touchscreens and brought the iPhone into existence. While numerous individuals perceived smartphones as constrained gadgets, Jobs foresaw a groundbreaking creation that merged a phone, an iPod, and an internet communicator. His imaginative perspective opened doors to unprecedented opportunities, reshaping the tech landscape and altering our relationship with technology.

Consider Post-it Notes, a creation brought to life by the innovative minds of Art Fry and Spencer Silver at 3M. Silver created a low-tack adhesive, yet Fry recognized its true potential as a bookmark, leading to the product's ultimate realization. Their imaginative perspective and implementation of the "look-and-key principle" transformed a seemingly mundane adhesive into a remarkable and essential office staple.

These examples demonstrate that we can achieve remarkable outcomes by acknowledging and engaging with potential. The "look-and-key principle" illustrates that our perception holds equal importance to our actions in bringing our creative visions to life, empowering us to innovate and elevate the mundane to the remarkable.

4. The University of Practical Experience: Learning from the Masters

Understudy to Mastery: The journey to creative mastery transcends mere formal education; it is enriched by the profound insights gained from effective mentorship, which are essential to achieving success. The "University of Practical Experience" concept embodies the collection of insights gained through observation and engagement with the wisdom of industry thought leaders. Through the journey of becoming an exceptional learner, we immerse ourselves in the myriad challenges and triumphs of the creative process, which invigorates our artistic expression.

It is an understanding that goes beyond mere words, emerging as a deep, intuitive grasp cultivated through keen observation and a genuine desire to absorb the subtle lessons imparted by the "master's whisper"—the quiet revelations from lived experience. This hands-on experience offers invaluable insights that can significantly enhance our creative development. It enhances our capabilities through insights gathered from those who have paved the way, encountered challenges, and attained success.

Reflect on Pablo Picasso's evolution. He learned from numerous artists before cultivating his distinctive approach. The period Picasso spent in his father's studio as an art professor and his subsequent engagements with fellow artists in Barcelona and Paris played a crucial role in developing his artistic vision. These experiences equipped him with the practical wisdom and motivation to explore new horizons and redefine the essence of art.

Consider the apprenticeship model found within the culinary realm. Renowned culinary figures such as Gordon Ramsay and Julia Child dedicated years to studying under master chefs, immersing themselves in techniques, and grasping the complexities of the culinary arts. This practical engagement enabled them to hone their abilities, cultivate distinctive approaches, and attain expertise.

These instances underscore the importance of the "University of Practical Experience" for fostering creative development. Through the wisdom of those who have come before us, we uncover profound understandings that elevate our skills and steer us on the path to excellence. This blend of practical understanding, alongside our enthusiasm and creativity, elevates us to unprecedented levels of achievement.

5. The Unwavering Spirit: The Will and the Way

The Synergistic Partnership: Creative vision flourishes through the synergistic partnership of two formidable forces— the unwavering determination to work and the spark of inspiration that propels one to transcend expectations. This remarkable partnership fuels our imaginative pursuits and steers us through ordinary and difficult times. Cultivating a motivated and dynamic mindset is fundamentally anchored in perseverance and self-discipline. It is the commitment to consistently fulfilling our responsibilities, even when inspiration feels absent.

Reflect on the journey of Thomas Edison, whose relentless determination embodies the essence of perseverance and innovation. His unwavering dedication to experimenting with countless materials before finding the perfect filament for the electric lightbulb exemplifies an extraordinary commitment to the pursuit of innovation. Edison's flashes of insight and enthusiasm for innovation sustained his creative spirit, culminating in one of history's most pivotal inventions.

Consider the artistic journey of Frida Kahlo, where her unwavering resolve and enthusiasm propelled her creative expression, even in the face of physical suffering and personal challenges. Kahlo's unwavering dedication, daily engagement with her craft, and moments of profound creativity led to a collection of work that remains enchanting and motivating. Her steadfast determination enabled her to articulate her distinctive perspective, crafting works of art that connect deeply with global audiences.

The motivation to go the extra mile often manifests as surges of passion and enthusiasm that ignite our creative impulses. These are called "two arms" as they synergistically support and propel us along our creative path. Cultivation of will and inspiration allows us to adeptly maneuver through challenges and realize our creative aspirations with steadfast resolve.

VI. Sustaining and Expanding Creative Impact:

1. The Untamed Muse: Wielding Creative Power with Caution

The Power Paradox: The essence of original thought is incredibly potent; it contains the capacity to mold our reality and impact the environment. Thus, creative vision possesses a "devastating power," yet it can be directed toward constructive endeavors to foster positive change. Essential elements include fostering a positive perspective and directing our imaginative forces towards objectives that serve individual fulfillment and the greater good of the community.

Reflect on the case of Henry Ford, who tapped into the essence of innovation to transform the automotive landscape. Ford's introduction of the assembly line democratized car ownership and revolutionized manufacturing practices in numerous sectors. His imaginative perspective held a significant influence, transforming the world of transportation and the economic landscape. Ford harnessed this influence with a sense of responsibility, directing efforts toward developing products that enhanced individual well-being and fostered societal advancement.

Consider the example of Nikola Tesla, whose groundbreaking contributions to electrical engineering held the promise of transforming our reality. Tesla's vision for wireless energy transmission and alternating current (AC) power systems exemplified the profound impact of innovative thinking. In the face of myriad challenges, Tesla's unwavering dedication to channeling his innovative vision for the collective benefit has forged a profound legacy that persists in shaping contemporary technology and energy paradigms.

These instances underscore the necessity of exercising creative influence with mindfulness and accountability. By fostering a hopeful perspective and channeling our efforts towards meaningful objectives, we can harness the transformative potential of imaginative thinking to create beneficial change for ourselves and the broader community.

2. The Ripple Effect: A Legacy Forged in Imagination

The Torchbearer: A creative vision transcends limitations; what remains is a legacy that persists through time. Our creative endeavors reshape regulations, organizations, and societal conventions. Creative imagination serves as the foundation of advancement, as it uniquely paves the way for evolution and sheds light on the journey toward a brighter future. We act as guides, illuminating the path for future generations to thrive in a more creative and uplifting realm.

Contemplate the lasting influence of Leonardo da Vinci, whose groundbreaking contributions to art, science, and engineering continue to inspire and drive us forward. Da Vinci's creative vision, reflected in iconic works such as the "Mona Lisa" and "The Last Supper," along with his myriad inventions and scientific inquiries, has profoundly influenced the trajectory of human advancement. His visionary thinking surpassed the limitations of his time, laying the groundwork for future advancements and exploration.

Consider the profound influence of Dr. Martin Luther King Jr., whose aspirations for civil rights and social justice transformed the fabric of society. King's visionary perspective on nonviolent resistance and his compelling oratory, exemplified by "I Have a Dream," persistently motivated global movements advocating for equality and human rights. His imaginative perspective established the foundation for meaningful societal transformation, inspiring countless individuals to pursue a fairer, more inclusive reality.

These examples demonstrate how imaginative foresight establishes an enduring impact, reshaping cultural standards and laying the groundwork for advancement. As guiding lights, we possess the chance to motivate and illuminate the journeys of those who follow in our footsteps. By embracing our creative imagination, we enhance a more vibrant, innovative world, and brimming with limitless potential.

VII.   Diving into the Wellspring of Imagination:

1.   Mental Retreat: Conversations in the Quiet

Solitude's Hour: Initiate your creative exploration through a retreat into solitude. Seek a serene environment, free from interruptions, and immerse yourself in profound dialogue with your inner self. This is not a mere surface-level examination; it is an exploration of your inner landscape, inviting you to engage with the desires and aspirations that reside within you.

Envision a serene space, bathed in sunlight, where you hold a journal, or perhaps picture yourself meandering through nature, letting your thoughts cascade effortlessly. This experience is truly unparalleled in the journey of self-exploration. During these serene moments of reflection, you have the opportunity to delve into your passions and aspirations, unraveling your truest desires. Engaging in this level of self-reflection marks the initial phase of creativity, offering insight and guidance for your aspirations.

Reflect on the act of journaling as embraced by individuals such as Virginia Woolf, who recognized the importance of solitude in nurturing her creative journey. Woolf's solitude allowed her to explore her inner landscape, leading to significant literary creations that still echo in contemporary discourse. Her serene contemplation played a crucial role in molding and expressing her perspective through impactful writing.

Consider Albert Einstein's reflective walks. He frequently credited his breakthroughs to moments spent in solitude, contemplating and permitting his thoughts to meander. These instances of solitude granted Einstein the insight essential for formulating his revolutionary theories, highlighting the significance of serene reflection in the creative process.

These instances emphasize the importance of a mental retreat, free from distractions, in revealing your authentic passions and desires. This serene reflection establishes the foundation for your imaginative perspective, steering you towards purposeful and inspired endeavors.

2. Inner Dialogue: Unmasking Desires

Self-Questioning: Engaging in self-questioning allows us to delve deep into our inner selves, initiating a transformative journey of self-discovery. Participate in a sincere and open conversation with your inner self, carefully uncovering the depths of your mind to reveal your truest aspirations. What genuinely ignites the passion within you? What ignites the limitless fires of your creativity?

Grasping your fundamental motivations is essential; it establishes a robust basis for a meaningful and intentional creative path. When you harmonize your aspirations with your innermost yearnings, you create a pathway for your endeavors to reflect your authentic self. This journey is known as "understanding the essence of personal needs," highlighting the crucial significance of acknowledging and valuing your deepest desires and ambitions. Engaging in this practice allows you to direct your creative energy towards a path that holds significance and brings fulfillment. Welcome this inner conversation, allowing it to lead you on a genuine, inspired creation journey.

Reflect on the practice of Frida Kahlo, whose profoundly personal art emerged from her inner dialogue and contemplation. Kahlo's paintings serve as a profound exploration of her deepest desires, suffering, and sense of self, resulting in creations that are both deeply personal and widely relatable. Her art embodies the profound journey of introspection and aligning one's aspirations with genuine passions.

Another illustration is Steve Jobs's introspective path, which often delved into self-examination to grasp his fundamental drives. Jobs' capacity to delve into his inner self and align with his true aspirations resulted in the development of innovative products at Apple. His connection to his vision and passions enabled him to harness his creative energy in a meaningful way, leading to groundbreaking innovations that reshaped the tech industry.

These examples demonstrate that we can harmonize our vision with our most profound aspirations through sincere self-reflection and revealing our authentic desires. This alignment enables us to engage in genuine and meaningful creation, steering us toward a journey of inspired expression.

3. Blueprinting the Ascent: Charting the Course

Plan in Motion: With your goal clearly defined, it's essential to chart the course for your creative expedition. This action plan will guide you through the journey's unavoidable fluctuations. Deconstruct your journey into manageable, attainable milestones, emphasizing the tools and abilities essential for each phase.

For example, if you aspire to craft a novel, start by mapping your narrative. Define specific milestones for the completion of each chapter and create a regular writing routine. When embarking on the journey of launching a business, it's essential to thoughtfully consider the foundational steps. Begin with thorough market research to understand your audience and competition. Follow this by ensuring proper business registration to establish legitimacy. Next, focus on product development to create something valuable. Finally, devise effective marketing strategies to communicate your offerings to the world.

This approach is known as "drafting a plan," as it involves transforming your vision into tangible actions that will manifest it into reality. Your roadmap serves as a living framework, adapting to your journey and ensuring you remain centered, inspired, and aligned with your creative goals.

Reflect on the path taken by J.K. Rowling in crafting the Harry Potter series. Rowling engaged in a thoughtful and intentional process, carefully crafting her narrative, shaping character journeys, and establishing key benchmarks for her writing. This systematic strategy enabled her to navigate the intricacies of her story and ultimately realize her artistic aspirations. Through a thoughtful dissection of her approach into achievable stages, she adeptly maneuvered the complexities of crafting a multi-book series, ultimately attaining worldwide acclaim.

Consider the strategic foresight demonstrated by Elon Musk in SpaceX's planning. Musk presents a comprehensive blueprint for the journey into space, outlining key achievements in rocket innovation, launch sequences, and the ambitious goal of sending humans to Mars. This innovative framework has steered SpaceX through various obstacles and progressions, turning the dream of interplanetary travel into a concrete reality.

These examples demonstrate the essential nature of crafting a roadmap to transform vision into tangible action. Creating a structured plan with specific, actionable steps empowers you to traverse your journey with assurance, fostering consistent advancement toward your creative aspirations.

4. Immediate Action: The Spark of Affirmation

The New Imperative: Action serves as the spark that ignites affirmation. Procrastination emerges as a formidable adversary to creativity, subtly stealing away our inherent potential. Embrace the now as your opportunity for growth; act with intention and begin your journey, regardless of the size of your first step. This first step creates a ripple effect, driving you onward and enhancing your self-assurance and faith in your aspirations.

Recognizing that "immediate action is the key to affirmation" is essential, as it highlights the necessity of transcending inertia. Embracing that essential initial move liberates us from the confines of doubt, turning aspirations into concrete experiences. Remember that every great journey starts with that first step—fully engage with the present moment and allow it to ignite your creative expression.

Reflect on the case of Sir Richard Branson, who embarked on his entrepreneurial journey by launching a student magazine at just 16 years old. Branson's prompt action on his idea set the stage for the emergence of the Virgin Group, a worldwide brand that spans multiple industries. His proactive mindset and readiness to embrace opportunities were pivotal in his journey toward entrepreneurial achievement.

Consider the narrative of Malala Yousafzai, who, in the face of life-threatening peril, courageously stepped forward to champion the cause of girls' education. Malala's bravery in standing up for her convictions at a young age thrust her into the international arena and resulted in meaningful progress in the realm of education advocacy. Her swift response and unwavering resolve serve as a beacon of inspiration for countless individuals across the globe.

These instances illustrate that the essence of the present moment resides in our capacity to make bold choices. Embracing the present moment and taking that initial step allows us to spark our creative potential, turning our visions into tangible realities.

5. The Reciprocity Principle: Giving and Receiving

The Equation of Life: The universe functions according to a fundamental truth—the principle of Reciprocity. The energy you project into the universe will ultimately return to you in some form. When you extend outstanding service to others, you cultivate the potential for them to respond with their gestures of kindness and support. This continuous act of generosity enriches those in your vicinity and fosters a profound sense of abundance and potential within your own creative pursuits.

Embracing this principle invites us to recognize that generosity and service are powerful catalysts for collective growth. When you share generously and purposefully, you initiate a ripple that enriches the experiences of those around you, ultimately bringing a positive reflection back to your path. The concept of this "life equation" highlights the profound interconnectedness of our actions and the limitless possibilities that emerge from a heart-centered perspective. Connect with the world through a lens of abundance, and observe how the cosmos reflects the vibrations you emit.

Reflect on Bill and Melinda Gates' altruistic endeavors via their foundation. Through their generous contributions to initiatives such as global health, education, and poverty alleviation, they have fostered a cycle of positive influence that has uplifted millions. Their dedication to service has profoundly improved the lives of those they assist while motivating others to engage in significant endeavors, fostering a ripple effect of kindness and development.

Consider the narrative of Muhammad Yunus, the visionary behind Grameen Bank, who innovatively introduced microfinance to elevate individuals from the grips of poverty. By providing small loans to individuals excluded from conventional banking systems, Yunus enabled people to initiate entrepreneurial ventures and enhance their quality of life. This act of service initiated a cycle of reciprocity, where those who received the loans embraced new opportunities to contribute to their communities, nurturing collective growth and prosperity.

These examples demonstrate that when we adopt the principle of reciprocity and interact with the world through a lens of generosity, we initiate a profound ripple effect. The energy we invest in our endeavors circles back to us, enriching our creative paths and fostering a more interconnected and abundant existence.

6. From Spark to Flame: Materializing Ideas

Ink on Paper: Our minds are filled with untapped concepts, each a possible spark of creativity that is eager to be realized. It's time to infuse these ideas with vitality, turning the abstract into the concrete. What is the initial move? Articulate your thoughts in written form. Let your mind mold and solidify these ideas into tangible, practical concepts.

Envisioning your concepts acts as a catalyst for your aspirations—it fuels the flame and transforms them into something tangible and achievable. This process is called "materializing on plans," highlighting the significance of turning abstract concepts into tangible, actionable strategies. By capturing your thoughts, you give them structure and depth, creating an environment for them to transform from simple ideas into powerful forces of success. Immerse yourself in your thoughts within the tangible realm and observe how they manifest right before you.

Reflect on Leonardo da Vinci's approach to sketching and note-taking. The multitude of sketches and notes he created, ranging from anatomical studies to engineering designs, was the foundation of his remarkable inventive spirit. By inscribing his thoughts onto paper, da Vinci transformed his visions into tangible forms, laying the groundwork for the extraordinary masterpieces and innovations that were to come.

Consider the storyboarding process utilized in filmmaking. Visionaries like Steven Spielberg engage in a thoughtful and deliberate process, crafting their cinematic narratives through intricate storyboards. These visual frameworks mold the narrative and steer the production journey, transforming intangible ideas into tangible strategies. Spielberg's talent for translating his visions onto paper has resulted in some of the most memorable films in cinema history.

These instances illustrate that when you articulate your thoughts in writing, you kindle the flame of your aspirations and pave the way for concrete success. Interacting with your concepts in the tangible realm enables them to materialize, evolving from simple reflections into concrete strategies that drive you forward on your path to achievement.

7. Mind-Altering Mantras: Fueling the Creative Furnace

The Power of Words: Words possess enormous power. They can reshape our perceptions and spark the flames of creativity. These transformative affirmations act as powerful catalysts for our imaginative spirit. Revisit, contemplate, and permit them to transform your internal dialogue, driving you toward your creative possibilities.

- **"Where there is no vision, the people perish."** This saying highlights the profound impact of a well-defined vision on one's transformation journey. It serves as an invitation to nurture a captivating vision that will steer our artistic pursuits.

A distinct vision serves as a guiding light, revealing the journey ahead and motivating us to progress with intention.

Reflect on Steve Jobs's path. His innovative mindset transformed entire sectors through technology. His distinct perspective on Apple informed his choices, resulting in groundbreaking products such as the iPhone and iPad that persistently influence our reality.

- **"Loss of money is unpleasant; loss of self-confidence is fatal to achievement."** This statement highlights the essential value of self-belief. Self-doubt stands as a significant barrier to the journey of creativity. Through the cultivation of self-assurance, we enable ourselves to navigate obstacles and realize our aspirations. Confidence in our capabilities ignites our imagination and determination.

Consider the journey of Oprah Winfrey, who navigated countless challenges with steadfast self-assurance. Her unwavering self-belief and clear vision propelled her to create a media empire, inspiring countless individuals and attaining extraordinary success.

- **"The combined wisdom and genius of mankind cannot argue against the liberty of thought."** This affirmation honors the strength found in autonomous thought. Originality serves as the foundation upon which creativity is built. By embracing unconventional ideas and daring to challenge the status quo, we unlock the limitless potential of our minds and create pathways for transformative innovation.

Albert Einstein's theories in physics questioned established norms and unveiled new dimensions of comprehension. His dedication to autonomous reasoning led to groundbreaking revelations that persistently shape the landscape of science today.

- **"Think before acting, not afterward."** Spontaneous action is a powerful catalyst for creativity, yet the significance of thoughtful planning cannot be overlooked. This statement reminds us to harmonize our motivated endeavors with thoughtful preparation. By thoughtfully reflecting on our actions, we can guarantee that our creative pursuits are imaginative and attainable.

  J.K. Rowling profoundly explored narrative structure, harmonizing the fluidity of inspiration with deliberate and strategic storytelling. This thoughtful method enabled her to weave a cohesive, engaging narrative that resonated with worldwide audiences.

Utilize the strength of these affirmations to ignite your imaginative spirit. Allow their insights to reshape your internal dialogue, propelling you onward with clarity, self-assurance, creativity, and intentionality. This is the journey of taking a mere thought and igniting it into a vibrant manifestation of creativity.

Warping Up: Unveiling the Mystery - A Spark to Ignite Generations

As we wrap up this journey into the realm of creative vision, we are reminded of the profound impact that self-reflection and purposeful action can have. Every thought, every spark of insight, acts as a fundamental component in the structure of our imaginative exploration. By exploring these thirty-five phases, we reveal the immense possibilities that lie within, enabling our inner creators to thrive and our aspirations to manifest.

Allow these stages to serve as the guiding light as you navigate the intricate pathways of your mind. Embrace the complex interplay of introspection and initiative, for it is within this space that the foundations of greatness are established. As you journey along this path, remember that each step taken, each act of creation, contributes to the ongoing narrative of human advancement.

In this limitless journey of creativity, we are not merely crafting our paths but playing a vital role in a shared future that overflows with potential and hope. United, we serve as beacons of creativity, guiding future generations toward new horizons. The exploration of creative vision transcends individual ambition; it stands as a profound affirmation of the resilience inherent in the human experience. Fully embrace it, allowing your imagination to shape the marvels of what lies ahead.

THE CRUCIBLE OF CREATION: FORGING STARTUPS FROM THE VOID

💰💰💰

The Vanquishing of Barriers: Paving the Path to Potential

This title shrouds the startup journey in a veil of mystery, hinting at the unknown challenges and triumphs that lie ahead. Entrepreneurs embark on a psychological quest, unlocking their inner potential and forging a path through the wilderness of possibility.

1. Visionary Foundations: Crafting the Compass

Harnessing Innate Potential. Every great startup has a visionary foundation, serving as an internal compass that guides entrepreneurs toward opportunities aligned with their deepest aspirations. It all begins with self-discovery: What problem are you uniquely positioned to solve? What value can you offer the world?

Think about an artist who spends years finding their unique style. This journey of self-discovery, rooted deep in the unconscious, often involves introspection and reflection.

Meditation, journaling, or quiet retreats can be powerful tools to uncover these hidden visions. For example, a writer might retreat to a secluded cabin, where, in the stillness, the central idea for a novel crystallizes. This solitude allows the subconscious mind to bring forth creative insights that may have been buried under daily distractions.

In the business world, consider the story of Steve Jobs and the founding of Apple. Jobs' frustrations with existing technology drove him to create products that were not only functional but beautifully designed. His vision was deeply rooted in a desire to change how people interacted with technology, and this passion became the driving force behind Apple's innovative spirit.

Another example is Sara Blakely, the founder of Spanx. Through her experiences, Blakely identified a problem and created a solution that revolutionized the shapewear industry. Her vision was born from personal necessity, and her relentless focus on solving that problem led to creating a billion-dollar company.

2. The Value Equation: Beyond the Myth of Easy Riches

Mutual Exchange as Growth's Keystone. As an entrepreneur, it's easy to fall for the myth of easy gains. Real and enduring value is a product of mutual exchange, not wishful thinking or oversight. Success demands sacrifices and commitments; you must be prepared to give something of value in return for what you want to gain.

This core psychological contract in the value equation is often grossly undervalued. Building a successful startup requires significant investment—not only financially but also in terms of time, energy, and emotional resilience. Inevitably, doubts and setbacks will arise to test your resolve. However, meeting these difficulties with a growth mindset can transform barriers into valuable learning experiences. This psychological alchemy is crucial for forging a lasting, meaningful venture.

Consider Elon Musk's journey. Musk's ventures, from Tesla to SpaceX, have faced numerous setbacks and challenges. Yet, his willingness to invest time, energy, and financial resources, coupled with his commitment to learning and adapting, has turned potential barriers into stepping stones for success. Musk's story underscores the importance of mutual exchange and persistent effort in creating enduring value.

Another example is Airbnb's rise. Founders Brian Chesky, Joe Gebbia, and Nathan Blecharczyk faced initial rejection and financial struggles. They had to make sacrifices and commit to their vision, offering significant value to hosts and guests. Their persistence and willingness to learn from setbacks ultimately transformed Airbnb into a global hospitality giant, illustrating the power of the value equation.

On a personal level, Oprah Winfrey's story highlights the importance of mutual exchange. Her journey from a challenging childhood to becoming a media mogul involved immense personal investment and resilience. She continually offered value through her authentic storytelling and empathetic approach, creating a lasting impact on millions of lives.

These examples demonstrate that true entrepreneurial success is not about easy riches but the continuous, reciprocal exchange of value by embracing this principle.

3. The Hero's Ascent: Embracing the Climb

There are no shortcuts to the Summit. Pursuing startup success is akin to embarking on an arduous yet rewarding climb. There are no shortcuts up the mountain of fulfillment. Difficulties are ever-present, acting as crucibles that test your resolve and dedication.

The psychological landscape of this journey is often treacherous. Self-doubt can be a constant nemesis, wielding negative self-talk and eroding confidence. The fear of failure looms large, potentially paralyzing one with indecision. Yet, some entrepreneurs undertake this heroic ascent with unyielding inner strength. They learn to harness a growth mindset, reframing obstacles into opportunities for further learning and adapting. This psychological fortitude propels them forward, one step at a time, toward promised land success.

Consider the journey of Howard Schultz, the former CEO of Starbucks. Schultz faced numerous rejections and setbacks when trying to convince investors of his vision to transform Starbucks from a coffee bean seller into a café chain. Despite these challenges, he remained steadfast, climbing the mountain step by step. His resilience and willingness to learn from failures ultimately led to Starbucks' global success.

Another example is the story of mountaineer Sir Edmund Hillary, one of the first to reach the summit of Mount Everest. His ascent was not only a physical challenge but also a psychological one, requiring immense determination and mental strength. Hillary's journey symbolizes the hero's ascent in the entrepreneurial world, where the climb is filled with physical and mental hurdles.

In the realm of technology, consider the story of Jeff Bezos and the early days of Amazon. Bezos faced significant obstacles, including financial struggles and skepticism about the viability of an online bookstore. Yet, his unwavering determination and ability to adapt and innovate turned

Amazon into one of the most successful companies in the world. Bezos' journey exemplifies the heroic ascent, where the path to success is fraught with challenges but ultimately rewarding.

These examples illustrate that embracing the climb with resilience and a growth mindset is crucial for entrepreneurial success. The journey may be challenging, but it is through overcoming these obstacles that true fulfillment and achievement are realized.

4. The Alchemy of Success: Intelligent Action and Timely Execution

Seasons of Success. The alchemy of success is a powerful mixture of intelligent action at the right time. Just as a skilled farmer understands the rhythm of nature, an entrepreneur must grasp the opportune moment to 'sow the seeds' of their vision. While careful planning is paramount, action paralyzed by over-intellectualization yields no harvest. The metaphor of "seasons of success" underscores the critical importance of timing and strategic action.

Consider the story of Airbnb. During the 2008 financial crisis, founders Brian Chesky, Joe Gebbia, and Nathan Blecharczyk recognized the perfect timing to launch their platform. As people sought ways to make extra income and travelers looked for affordable accommodation, Airbnb's concept resonated. Their intelligent action at this opportune moment transformed the startup into a global hospitality leader.

Another example is Apple's introduction of the iPhone in 2007. Steve Jobs and his team meticulously planned the product's launch, ensuring it was technologically advanced yet user-friendly. The timing was impeccable, aligning with a growing demand for multifunctional mobile devices. This strategic action at the right moment redefined the smartphone industry and set new standards for innovation.

In space exploration, SpaceX's successful launch of the Falcon Heavy rocket exemplifies the alchemy of success. Elon Musk's careful planning and intelligent execution, paired with an understanding of the right moment to demonstrate the rocket's capabilities, positioned SpaceX as a leader in the aerospace industry. The timing was crucial, coinciding with a renewed interest in space travel and exploration.

On a personal level, consider J.K. Rowling's journey. The timing of her release of the Harry Potter series during a period when young adult fiction was gaining popularity contributed significantly to its success. Her careful planning and strategic action in launching the series captured the imaginations of millions, leading to a global phenomenon.

These examples highlight that success is not merely a result of hard work and planning but also of executing actions at the right time. Entrepreneurs must cultivate the intuition to recognize their 'seasons of success' and act decisively to achieve their vision. By understanding and harnessing this alchemy, they can turn potential into reality and achieve remarkable success.

5. The Phoenix Principle: Rising from the Ashes of Self-Doubt

The fiercest battles are not fought in boardrooms or markets but within the corridors of the mind. An entrepreneur cannot master the external world until they have faced and overcome their inner demons. Self-doubt, a lingering shadow born of uncertainty and fear, can be an overwhelming adversary, threatening to cripple the spirit and stifle creativity.

This struggle is universal and requires an inner revolution—a dedication to self-awareness and personal growth. To rise from the ashes of self-doubt, one must embark on a journey of introspection, confronting the doubts and fears that lurk within. Through this courageous confrontation, the flames of self-doubt are extinguished, and the resilient spirit of the entrepreneur is reborn, like a phoenix rising anew.

Embrace the transformative power of self-awareness and growth. By nurturing your inner strength and fortitude, you can emerge stronger, more confident, and ready to conquer the challenges that lie ahead. The Phoenix Principle reminds us that from the ashes of our doubts, we can soar to new heights, guided by the light of our renewed self-belief.

a. Banishing the Shadows: A Mind Unbound

The first step to any psychological victory lies in liberating the mind from the bondage of self-doubt. While fear is a natural human emotion, it should never be the driving force. Meditation and mindfulness can train your mind to recognize intrusive thoughts and counter negativity. By consistently practicing these techniques, you build mental resilience and foster a mindset that is free, focused, and unencumbered by doubt.

Consider the example of tennis champion Serena Williams. Known for her mental toughness, Williams uses mindfulness and meditation to stay focused and resilient on the court. Her ability to banish self-doubt and maintain a strong mental game has been crucial to her success.

b. The Inventory of Self: Assessing Your Arsenal

Self-awareness is the foundation of sustainable success. Conduct a thorough inventory of your knowledge bases, experiences, and innate talents. What is your unique value proposition? This internal assessment will illuminate your strengths and reveal the opportunities that align perfectly with your passions. Understanding your capabilities allows you to leverage them effectively, ensuring your pursuits are ambitious and attainable.

Take, for example, Oprah Winfrey's rise to success. She built an empire centered around her strengths by thoroughly understanding her unique ability to connect with people and tell compelling stories. Her self-awareness and ability to assess her talents allowed her to create opportunities aligned with her passions.

c. **The Quest for Relevance: Seeking the Marketplace**

Armed with self-awareness, you are prepared to embark on the quest for relevance. Identify where your unique abilities can most benefit your marketplace or ideal customer. This target audience becomes your guiding star in building a startup. The principle of going the extra mile elevates the ordinary to the extraordinary. This relentless dedication and effort distinguish successful entrepreneurs from the rest in business. You solidify your relevance by consistently exceeding expectations and delivering exceptional value, carving out your place in the market.

Consider the story of Howard Schultz and Starbucks. Schultz identified a gap in the market for a coffeehouse experience that provided more than just coffee. He transformed Starbucks into a global brand by leveraging his understanding of consumer desires and going the extra mile to create a welcoming environment.

These steps illustrate the transformative journey of the Phoenix Principle. By overcoming self-doubt, assessing your unique strengths, and striving for relevance, you can rise from the ashes of uncertainty and achieve entrepreneurial success.

6. The Extra Mile Principle: Unlocking the Hidden Reserves

Beyond the Expected. The Extra Mile Principle functions like an ancient alchemical formula, transforming average effort into extraordinary success. Pushing beyond conventional limits unlocks hidden reserves of creativity, resilience, and determination within the entrepreneur. While the concept may sound straightforward, mastering its application is the hallmark of those who rise above mediocrity.

Embracing the Extra Mile Principle means committing beyond what is required or expected. It's about finding that extra reserve of effort, that hidden spark of innovation, and that untapped well of perseverance. This principle unlocks something almost magical within—an element of mystery and romance that elevates ordinary tasks into extraordinary achievements.

a. The Alchemy of Effort

Consider it an alchemical process, where the raw materials of hard work, dedication, and passion are transmuted into the gold of success. The Extra Mile Principle requires more than just additional effort; it demands a mindset shift, a willingness to explore uncharted territories, and an embrace of the unknown. By doing so, you tap into hidden potentials that were previously dormant.

Think about the story of Thomas Edison. Despite thousands of failures, his relentless pursuit and extra effort in perfecting the light bulb epitomizes the alchemy of effort. Edison's ability to push beyond conventional limits and persist through adversity transformed his vision into reality, creating one of the most significant inventions in history.

b. The Journey of Transformation

Adopting the Extra Mile Principle suggests a journey of transformation. Each step taken beyond the ordinary is a step towards self-discovery and growth. The road is not easy, but it is paved with opportunities to learn, innovate, and excel. This journey is unique to each individual, and the challenges faced along the way only serve to strengthen resolve and sharpen skills.

Consider Oprah Winfrey's journey. From her humble beginnings to becoming a global media mogul, Oprah's commitment to going the extra mile in her work and personal growth has been instrumental in her success. Her transformative journey is a testament to the power of perseverance and continuous self-improvement.

c. The Hallmark of Excellence

The hallmark of those who master this principle is their relentless pursuit of excellence. They understand that true success is not just about reaching the destination but about the journey itself. The Extra Mile Principle is a testament to their unwavering commitment, ability to persevere in adversity, and dedication to continuous improvement.

d. Embracing the Unknown

Unlocking hidden reserves is not just about working harder; it's about working smarter. It involves strategic thinking, innovative problem-solving, and a fearless approach to challenges. By pushing beyond the expected, you achieve greater results and inspire those around you to elevate their efforts.

Steve Jobs' approach to innovation at Apple exemplifies this principle. His willingness to embrace the unknown and push the boundaries of what was possible led to the creation of groundbreaking products like the iPhone and the Mac. Jobs' relentless pursuit of excellence and innovation set new standards in the technology industry.

In the end, the Extra Mile Principle is more than just a strategy; it's a philosophy. It's a way of life that celebrates the power of going beyond the ordinary, embracing the extraordinary, and unlocking the limitless potential within. Ready to embark on this transformative journey? The road to excellence awaits.

The Awakening of Success Consciousness: Unveiling the Alchemist Within

In the hidden recesses of the mind lies a profound ability—the power to transmute ordinary ambition into extraordinary success. This awakening of success consciousness is akin to unveiling the alchemist within, a journey of transformation where raw potential is turned into golden achievement. The mysterious allure of this title hints at the almost magical capability that developing a success mindset can bestow upon us.

With each step, we implement strategies that interweave the rich themes of psychology, forging a path through the labyrinth of self-doubt and emerging into the light of self-empowerment. By understanding and harnessing the hidden forces within our minds, we can unlock an uncharted realm of possibilities, guiding our aspirations toward tangible realities. Prepare to embark on this transformative journey as we reveal the alchemical secrets that lie within and awaken the consciousness of success.

1. The Purpose-Driven Life: Beyond the Horizon

Cultivating a Definitive Aim: A new horizon appears when the extra mile has been mastered. Attention is no longer required for mere effort but must be transferred to cultivating a definitive aim. This awakening of success consciousness demands that you crystallize your purpose and translate it into a concrete plan.

The journey is not about attracting favorable attention or external validation; it's about discovering your guiding ambition, your North Star that will illuminate your path. Conquering the extra mile reveals a new horizon, shifting the focus from sheer effort to developing a clear-cut purpose.

Awakening your success consciousness is akin to an ancient alchemical formula—the lead of undirected effort transformed into the gold of focused ambition. This inner alchemy requires deep self-reflection to uncover your central values and the impact you wish to leave on the world.

By engaging in this profound introspection, you discover the hidden wellspring of purpose within you. This crystallized purpose becomes the bedrock of your journey, guiding your actions with unwavering clarity. Your purpose-driven life is not merely a pursuit of goals but a harmonious alignment of your ambitions with your deepest values, creating a lasting legacy that transcends the ordinary.

Embrace this inner alchemy, and let your purpose be the beacon that guides you beyond the horizon. The world awaits the unique mark you are destined to leave, forged through the fire of self-discovery and the gold of focused ambition.

2. The Blueprint of Ambition: The Elixir of Service

Service as the Foundation: In the grand architecture of your ambitions, service must be the cornerstone upon which everything else is built. True fulfillment stems from uplifting others, from offering your unique gifts and talents to the world in a way that transforms and enriches lives. Your definitive plan should be a direct expression of who you are and what you are capable of contributing.

The term "service one has for sale" can feel cold and transactional, so let's reframe it as the "Elixir of Service." This metaphor elevates your offerings to something almost magical—a transformative essence that brings value not only to those you serve but also to yourself. By providing this elixir, you create a cycle of enrichment where your contributions ignite the potential in others and simultaneously fuel your sense of purpose.

Service becomes the base of your blueprint, grounding your ambitions in a cause greater than yourself. Real satisfaction arises from this act of giving as you dedicate yourself to something bigger; intrinsic motivation naturally follows, propelling you forward on your entrepreneurial journey. The Elixir of Service is not just a gift to the world; it's a vital source of internal fire, driving you to achieve your goals with passion and integrity.

This transformational approach ensures that your ambitions are successful and deeply fulfilling, as they resonate with your core values and the impact you wish to leave on the world. Let the Elixir of Service guide your path, turning your vision into a reality that benefits all.

3. The Principles of Triumph: The Alchemist's Toolkit

Adaptability in Action: The path to purpose is rife with unexpected challenges. Just as the alchemist possesses a toolkit of techniques for transformation, you, too, must arm yourself with the principles of achievement. Adaptability becomes your secret weapon, enabling you to navigate any terrain your purpose requires you to tread.

Imagine yourself as a psychological alchemist, wielding the principles of triumph like mystical incantations to overcome obstacles. Adaptability will be your trump card, turning uncharted land into a conquerable domain. Building resilience, resourcefulness, and strategic thinking transforms potential defeats into stepping stones on the path to success.

Mastering these principles ensures that you are prepared for the ever-changing landscape of your journey. With each challenge, you refine your skills, becoming more adept at handling the unforeseen and turning adversity into opportunity. This toolkit is not merely a collection of techniques; it is a dynamic arsenal, constantly evolving with your experiences and growth.

Embrace the alchemical journey, for within these principles lies the power to transmute the ordinary into the extraordinary. Equip yourself with this toolkit, and you will find that the triumphs of your purpose are well within your reach. Ready to forge ahead with your alchemist's toolkit? The adventure awaits.

4. The Tenacity of Spirit: Forging the Armor of Resilience

Persistence in the Face of Adversity: A mind steeped in success consciousness develops unwavering tenacity.

Challenges do not dampen one's spirit but rather fortify it to face adversity boldly. Imagine being clothed in armor—persistence—that protects you from the onslaught of life's trials.

The concept of "mind preparation" can seem vague, so we envision "forging the armor of resilience" to create a more evocative and powerful image. This armor is not bestowed upon you but forged through the relentless flames of challenge and hardship. The more obstacles you overcome, the stronger your psychological muscles become, solidifying your belief that you can eventually attain your dreams.

Success consciousness imparts to the mind an ever-increasing tenacity. Challenges are not met with despair but with a relentless spirit. In your persistence lies your armor, a shield that shelters you from the assaults of adversity. This armor is forged in the fire of trials, each difficulty strengthening your resolve and fortitude.

As you conquer each challenge, your doubts and fears begin to dissolve, replaced by an unshakable belief in your capabilities. The process of forging this armor is transformative, inviting you on a journey of self-discovery and purpose. Through this journey, you emerge not just as a survivor but as a resilient and triumphant individual, ready to face any storm with unwavering determination.

Embrace the Tenacity of Spirit and let it forge your armor of resilience. The trials you face are not setbacks but opportunities to strengthen your resolve and reinforce your path toward success. Ready to wear your armor and face the world with newfound strength? The adventure awaits.

5. The Attitude of Giving: The Alchemical Exchange

Service Before Self: The ancient alchemists understood the law of sacred exchange—a principle that goes beyond mere transactions. True wealth is not measured by what you accumulate but by the value you bring to the world through your service. Shifting your focus from getting to giving is a fundamental step toward awakening success consciousness.

We refer to this as the "Alchemical Exchange" to evoke a sense of mystery and transformation. By prioritizing service, you engage in a profound process in which your gifts and talents become catalysts for personal fulfillment and prosperity.

This mental shift from self-centered pursuits to service-oriented goals fosters a transformative journey. Through your contributions, you initiate an exchange that enriches both the giver and the receiver. This alchemical process realizes your true potential, and your efforts yield far greater rewards than material gain alone.

Embracing the Attitude of Giving means recognizing that every act of service is a step toward creating a meaningful and impactful legacy. Your talents and gifts, when shared generously, ignite a cycle of abundance that nourishes your spirit and enhances the lives of others. This is the essence of the Alchemical Exchange—a journey where giving becomes the means to unlocking your highest potential and achieving lasting success.

Ready to embrace this transformative principle? Let your service be the alchemy that turns your aspirations into golden reality.

6. The Indispensable Factor: The Philosopher's Stone

Making Oneself Essential: Alchemists sought the philosopher's stone in ancient lore, a fabled substance believed to transmute base metals into gold. In the modern sense, becoming indispensable through valuable service is akin to discovering your philosopher's stone. It is more than a key to financial abundance; it is the mainspring of a deeply and richly lived life.

Making oneself essential involves offering irreplaceable value. This transcends mere economic gain and taps into the profound impact you can have on those around you. By consistently providing exceptional service and demonstrating unique qualities, you become a linchpin in your field, someone others depend on and seek out.

This transformation from ordinary to extraordinary propels individuals beyond the realm of mediocrity. In this context, the philosopher's stone symbolizes the ultimate achievement of making oneself indispensable through unwavering dedication, skill, and a commitment to excellence. It is the essence of living a life that not only thrives on personal success but also enriches the lives of others. This is the path to true fulfillment, where every action resonates with purpose and significance.

7. The Symphony of Synergy: The Alchemical Chorus

Harmonizing Interactions: Success consciousness recognizes that, ultimately, people empower people. Harmonious relationships form the bedrock upon which synergy stands. Just as an orchestra generates a powerful sound from the combined talents of its members, a team of people can achieve remarkable feats when working together in harmony.

The concept of "negotiation with others with minimum friction" is vital, but let's delve deeper. We introduce the term "Alchemical Chorus" to evoke a sense of mystery and collaboration. Perfecting the collaboration craft, like an alchemist transmuting lead into gold, transforms interactions into something extraordinary.

Forging strong relationships within this alchemical chorus means understanding and valuing each person's contributions. It's about creating a symphony where each note complements the others, resulting in a harmonious and powerful collective performance. This synergy is not just about working together but about creating an environment where everyone thrives and succeeds.

Nurturing these connections and mastering the art of collaboration turns your network into your greatest asset. This harmonious synergy amplifies each individual's potential, making the collective far greater than the sum of its parts. The alchemical chorus is a transformative process that turns ordinary interactions into golden opportunities for growth and success. Embrace this Symphony of Synergy and let the alchemical chorus guide your interactions. You and your connections can achieve remarkable things together, creating a legacy of collaboration and triumph.

8. The Bedrock of Success: The Philosopher's Elixir

The Extra Mile Ethos: Confidence and cooperation are the two-fold elixirs brewed in the cauldron of success consciousness. This potent mix is the fire within, fueling the positive fight of will and perseverance. Synergistic cooperation, embodying principles like the Golden Rule, fosters camaraderie that magnifies your efforts and achievements.

The notion of "confidence and friendship acquisition" may sound transactional, so let's focus instead on "self-belief" and "cooperation" for a more psychologically enriching frame. By adopting the ethos of going the extra mile, you cultivate mutual respect and benefit, laying a solid foundation for your alchemical enterprise.

This extra-mile ethos is about more than effort—it's about embracing a mindset that values collective upliftment and personal growth. It acknowledges that true success is interwoven with the success of others. By pushing beyond the expected and fostering a cooperative spirit, you unlock reservoirs of potential within yourself and those around you.

The Philosopher's Elixir transforms these principles into a powerful formula for success. It is a testament to the transformative power of a positive mindset and collaborative effort. Through this alchemical journey, you can build a career and legacy of meaningful impact and enduring success.

Embrace the Philosopher's Elixir and let it guide your path. The fire of self-belief and the strength of cooperation are your keys to unlocking a future where success is not just achieved but profoundly shared and deeply fulfilling.

SECTION 4: THE CRUCIBLE OF CREATION

CREATIVE VISION WARNINGS

&❧ &❧ &❧

In the dynamic realm of human advancement, imaginative thinking serves as both a guidepost for new directions and a warning against old dangers. Even though creative thinking propels societies ahead, it is not without its dangers and must be handled with caution. Because of the two sides to every coin, creative vision requires moderation, keeping an eye out for both the benefits and drawbacks of pursuing innovative ideas. We must listen to the cautions that come with our boldest aspirations as we explore this intriguing idea further and find out how inspiration and accountability interact delicately.

Eluded Creative Vision – Waring of the Abyss of the Visionary's Psyche

Peering into the abyss of the visionary's psyche reveals a landscape of profound complexity and paradox. The boundless optimism and relentless drive that propel creative visionaries can often teeter on the brink of obsession and delusion. This duality forms the crux of understanding the enigmatic nature of creative vision. By examining the delicate balance between unyielding ambition and the potential pitfalls of a visionary's zeal, we gain insight into the precarious tightrope that visionaries walk. This exploration highlights the thin line between brilliance and madness, optimism and mania, and the profound impact of their psyche on their creations and the world around them.

1. **Resilient Optimism - Transfer to Warning of Eluded Creative Vision**

Visionary optimism is often intertwined with a tinge of mania. Relentless pursuit of their vision can lead to obsession, pushing them down paths that others might deem illogical, even dangerous. This raises an intriguing question: Is the visionary's optimism a strength or a delusion? Perhaps the answer lies in the delicate balance between unwavering faith and the siren call of chasing shadows.

Consider Vincent van Gogh, whose optimism and creative hunger drove him to produce remarkable works of art despite his mental health struggles. His boundless optimism teetered on the edge of mania, yet it fueled his extraordinary creativity. Van Gogh's "Starry Night" is an illustration—painted while he was in a mental asylum, reflecting his intense passion and troubled mind. His vision was resilient, but it also consumed him.

Another example is Steve Jobs, who exhibited resilient optimism in the face of adversity. Despite numerous setbacks, jobs' relentless pursuit of his vision for Apple was his strength and his Achilles' heel. His unwavering belief in his ideas often bordered on obsession, yet it led to revolutionary products like the iPhone. Jobs walked the tightrope between visionary brilliance and the brink of obsession, illustrating the dual-edged nature of resilient optimism.

The story of J.K. Rowling is also worth mentioning. Her optimism and belief in her Harry Potter series kept her going through financial struggles and numerous rejections from publishers. Her resilient optimism eventually paid off, transforming her into one of the most successful authors of all time. However, the pressure and intense focus on her vision also took a toll on her mental health, highlighting the fine line between resilient optimism and potential psychological strain.

These examples illustrate that visionaries' optimism can be a powerful driving force, but it must be carefully balanced to avoid the abyss of obsession. Recognizing this balance is crucial for harnessing creative vision without succumbing to its darker aspects.

2. **Foresight and Leadership - Transfer to Warning of Eluded Creative Vision**

The source of a visionary's foresight is hotly debated. Is it a spark of brilliance in an otherwise unbalanced mind or heightened sensitivity to subtle currents of change? It's likely a complex interplay between intuition, experience, and a touch of the unorthodox.

Steve Jobs exemplifies this blend. His unique ability to foresee technological trends was remarkable, as he combined intuition with a profound understanding of market needs. His foresight, often seen as a mad genius, revolutionized multiple industries. The introduction of the iPhone in 2007 is a prime example. While many were skeptical, Jobs' vision of a touch-screen smartphone without a physical keyboard defied conventions and redefined communication, work, and entertainment. His leadership was a dance between chaos and order, innovation and practicality, creating a legacy of groundbreaking products.

Consider another example: Elon Musk. His foresight in multiple fields—space exploration, electric vehicles, and artificial intelligence—often appears as a mix of brilliance and eccentricity. Musk's leadership at SpaceX, for instance, saw the company achieve unprecedented feats like landing reusable rockets, a concept once deemed impossible by many. His sensitivity to technological shifts and unwavering drive highlights the complex nature of visionary foresight.

Then there's Nikola Tesla, whose foresight in electrical engineering laid the groundwork for many modern technologies. Despite facing numerous challenges and being seen as eccentric, Tesla's visionary ideas on alternating current (AC) power systems were revolutionary. His foresight blended deep scientific understanding and a relentless pursuit of innovation, often bordering on the unorthodox.

These examples illustrate that visionary foresight and leadership often stem from a complex interplay of factors. Recognizing this interplay allows us to appreciate the fine line between brilliance and madness, intuition and experience, ultimately harnessing these traits for transformative innovation.

3. **The Fire Within - Transfer to Warning of Eluded Creative Vision**

The depths of a visionary's desire can indeed be unnerving. Their relentless drive often raises questions about their ego and ambition. Are they genuinely motivated by a desire to improve the world, or is a narcissistic impulse at play? This ambiguity adds an element of mystery to their persona.

Elon Musk serves as a prime example. His relentless drive to push the boundaries of the known is both inspiring and controversial. Musk's ventures into electric cars, space travel, and neural technology are groundbreaking. However, his ambitions sometimes blur the line between genuine innovation and self-promotion. Take SpaceX's mission to colonize Mars: while it promises to advance human space exploration, some see it as an extension of Musk's larger-than-life persona. This duality—innovator versus self-promoter—adds complexity to his legacy.

Similarly, Howard Hughes is an aviator and film producer. Hughes' relentless pursuit of innovation in aviation and cinema was legendary, yet his obsessive drive often veered into the realm of the bizarre and self-destructive. His desire to build the largest aircraft of his time, the Spruce Goose, led to a project of immense ambition but limited practical success. Hughes' life embodies the paradox of the visionary's fire: blazing brilliance intertwined with personal demons.

On the other hand, Thomas Edison's fire drove him to over 1,000 patents, transforming industries with inventions like the electric light bulb. Yet Edison's aggressive business tactics, such as his rivalry with Tesla, also showcased an ego-driven aspect. His ambition and relentless pursuit of innovation were a double-edged sword, contributing to his success and the ethical quandaries that shadowed it.

These examples illustrate that the fire within a visionary can be both a source of inspiration and a cause for concern. The balance between genuine aspiration and egotistical drive defines the visionary's impact on the world and their journey through the abyss of their psyche.

4. Rewarding Initiative Transfer to Warning of Eluded Creative Vision

The relentless pursuit of progress can foster a culture where ambition pits immediate gain against the collective good. This raises an uncomfortable question: does the system that fuels creative vision also sow the seeds of its own undoing?

The tech industry offers a poignant example. Rapid innovation often comes at the cost of ethical considerations and social cohesion. The drive for progress can overshadow the broader impact on society, manifesting in issues like data privacy breaches and the instability of the gig economy.

Consider the case of Facebook. Its rapid growth and relentless pursuit of user engagement led to significant advancements in social connectivity. However, this progress came with a steep price—issues like data privacy violations and the platform's role in spreading misinformation raised serious ethical concerns. The system propelling Facebook to success also contributed to its most significant challenges, exemplifying the double-edged nature of rewarding initiatives.

Similarly, the gig economy, championed by companies like Uber and Lyft, epitomizes the tension between innovation and social impact. While these platforms revolutionized transportation and created new job opportunities, they also introduced a level of instability for workers. The lack of employee benefits and job security highlights the darker side of relentless ambition, where immediate gains for the company can come at the expense of worker well-being.

This paradox is also evident in the pharmaceutical industry. The push for rapid drug development and substantial profits has led to groundbreaking medical advancements. However, it has also resulted in ethical dilemmas, such as the opioid crisis in the United States. Pharmaceutical companies pursued aggressive marketing strategies for painkillers, leading to widespread addiction and societal harm. The drive for progress, in this case, had devastating consequences.

These examples underscore the importance of balancing ambition with ethical considerations. Entrepreneurs must recognize that the relentless pursuit of progress while rewarding, must be tempered with a commitment to the collective good. Only then can we harness creative vision without falling into the traps of its potential undoing.

5. The Power of Incentive - Transfer to Warning of Eluded Creative Vision

Incentives are indeed a double-edged sword. The profit motive can drive the ruthless pursuit of financial gain, often blurring ethical boundaries. In this relentless quest, the visionary may leave a trail of destruction in their wake, and the fine line between genius and ruthless ambition becomes dangerously thin, often concealed under the veil of self-justification and personal gain.

Consider the case of pharmaceutical companies prioritizing profit over patient well-being. The opioid crisis in the United States serves as a stark example. Companies like Purdue Pharma aggressively marketed opioids, downplaying the risks of addiction to maximize profits. This led to widespread misuse and a public health crisis, demonstrating how pursuing financial gain can have devastating societal impacts.

Another example is the tobacco industry. For decades, major tobacco companies have engaged in deceptive practices to minimize the health risks of smoking, driven by the profit motive. They prioritized sales over the well-being of consumers, leading to countless preventable deaths and long-term health issues.

On a different note, the banking industry also illustrates this point before the 2008 financial crisis. The aggressive pursuit of profits through risky lending practices and financial products led to a global economic meltdown. The incentives for short-term gains blinded many to the long-term consequences, showcasing the destructive potential of misaligned incentives.

The story of Uber's early years further highlights this duality. The drive for rapid growth and market dominance led to a culture where ethical boundaries were often overlooked. Reports of unfair labor practices, aggressive tactics against competitors, and internal misconduct painted a picture of ambition overshadowing ethical considerations. It wasn't until these issues were publicly scrutinized that significant changes were made to address the ethical lapses.

These examples underscore the need to balance the power of incentives with a strong ethical framework. Visionaries must be wary of the seductive lure of financial gain, which can compromise integrity. The true measure of success lies not just in profits but in the positive impact on society and adherence to ethical principles.

In Conclusion, by delving into the enigmatic depths of the visionary's psyche, we unravel the intricate forces that sculpt our world. Creative vision is a double-edged sword, a potent catalyst for immense progress and potential devastation. From resilient optimism, often bordering on mania, to the foresight seen as either mad genius or intuitive brilliance, visionaries walk a tightrope of ambition and innovation. Their relentless drive, sometimes fueled by a narcissistic impulse, poses the question of whether they push boundaries for collective good or personal gain. While rewarding, pursuing progress and incentives also risks fostering ethical and social dilemmas. Grasping the psychology of visionaries allows us to harness their formidable power for the greater good, channeling their brilliance to propel us forward while being mindful of the shadow they might cast.

The Derailers of Startup Transformation: Navigating the Labyrinth of Success

In the ever-evolving landscape of startups, navigating the labyrinth of success is critical. The journey from a mere idea to a flourishing enterprise is fraught with challenges and potential derailers. Understanding these pitfalls is essential to transforming visionary concepts into sustainable realities. By acknowledging and addressing the common obstacles startups face—ranging from leadership missteps to market misalignment—entrepreneurs can better prepare themselves to overcome hurdles and pave the way for innovation and growth. This exploration underscores the significance of foresight, adaptability, and ethical considerations in steering a startup toward enduring success.

1. The Illusion of Quick Riches: A Fata Morgana in the Desert

The mirage of quick riches is a tantalizing simulacrum that lures many entrepreneurs off the straight and narrow. Chasing these shadows is akin to pursuing an illusion, a shortcut to wealth that inevitably crashes into a sense of disillusionment. True fulfillment, much like an oasis in the desert, springs from the journey of creation itself.

Consider the story of the infamous dot-com bubble of the late 1990s. Startups flooded the market, fueled by the allure of instant wealth, only to see their dreams crumble as the bubble burst, leaving many in financial ruin. The lesson here is clear: superficial fulfillment is fleeting, and the quest for quick riches can be perilous.

The imagery of a desert mirage perfectly encapsulates this notion. Entrepreneurs must recognize that passion, purpose, and the sense of building something meaningful are the anchors that keep them grounded. These elements provide the satisfaction and resilience to persevere until sustainable success is achieved.

Take, for example, Amazon's journey. Jeff Bezos did not achieve success overnight. He persisted through years of unprofitability, driven by a clear vision and purpose. This tenacity and commitment to long-term goals rather than short-term gains ultimately led Amazon to become today's giant.

2. The Shortcut Mirage: The Siren Song of Deception

The siren song of shortcuts often proves difficult to withstand. Numerous diversions may appear to offer rapid advancement, yet they frequently guide us toward perilous paths. Engaging in shortcuts that involve unethical practices or dubious methods can lead entrepreneurs into legal complications and damage their reputations. This treacherous diversion embodies the concept of the "siren song of deceit," infusing complexity and psychological temptation into the equation of success.

Illustrative example: The case of Enron, a company once heralded as an innovative leader in the energy sector. Their reliance on deceptive accounting practices to maintain the appearance of profitability ultimately led to one of the most infamous corporate scandals in history. The shortcuts taken not only resulted in legal repercussions but also devastated the lives of employees and investors.

The most rewarding ventures are those built on solid foundations of integrity and ethical business practices. Consider the success of Patagonia, a company renowned for its commitment to ethical practices and sustainability. Patagonia has cultivated a loyal customer base by prioritizing values over shortcuts and sustained long-term growth.

The "siren song of shortcut mirage" is a powerful metaphor for the alluring yet dangerous appeal of unethical shortcuts. Entrepreneurs must remain vigilant, prioritizing integrity and ethical practices to navigate the labyrinth of success without falling prey to these deceptive detours.

3. The Forceful Claim: Slaying the Golden Goose

The Golden Goose Paradox is a poignant lesson for any entrepreneur tempted by forceful methods. The fable teaches us that exploiting a resource for temporary gain can lead to its destruction, extinguishing long-term value. This metaphor of "killing the golden goose" underscores the drastic consequences of trying to gain immediate desires through sheer force.

Take, for instance, the fast fashion industry. Companies prioritizing rapid production and short-term profits often exploit labor and environmental resources, ultimately leading to unsustainable practices and reputational damage. In contrast, brands like Patagonia have built trust and mutual benefits by focusing on sustainable practices and ethical production.

Building trust and nurturing mutually beneficial relationships are vital keys to sustainable success. Entrepreneurs must resist the siren call of quick gains through unethical practices and instead focus on creating lasting value. The revised edition of this concept adds a touch of mystery and psychological charm, urging readers to approach startup transformation with a cautious strategy and a clear ethical outlook.

The story of Henry Ford's success with the Model T is an example of sustainable innovation. Rather than cutting corners, Ford focused on improving production processes and building a reliable product, ensuring long-term success and revolutionizing the automobile industry.

4. The Boomerang of Deceit: Karma's Tangled Web

The Deceiver's Dilemma is a tale as old as time. Deception, no matter how cleverly disguised, inevitably backfires. Cunning gives cheaters a misplaced advantage, yet the result is often shame and a reputation tarnished beyond repair. This concept of "Karma's tangled web" adds a touch of mystery and emphasizes the inevitable repercussions of deceit.

Consider the story of Elizabeth Holmes and Theranos. The allure of groundbreaking innovation led to deceptive practices, which initially brought success but ultimately resulted in one of the biggest scandals in the healthcare industry. The deceitful foundation collapsed, leaving a trail of shattered trust and legal consequences.

Trust is earned by weaving a web of integrity that endures. A startup built on lies is like a castle made of sand, destined to be washed away by the waves of truth. Uber's CEO, Travis Kalanick, 's fall also illustrates this point. His aggressive, often unethical leadership approach eventually led to his ousting and a re-evaluation of the company's culture and practices.

Building a lasting enterprise demands honesty and transparency. Entrepreneurs must recognize that deceit is a short-lived strategy with long-term consequences. Embracing ethical practices fosters trust and paves the way for sustainable success, avoiding the tangled web of karma.

5. The Gossip Mill: Navigating the Maelstrom of Misinformation

The Whisperers in the Dark: Unveiling the Machinery of Rumors. A startup could be crippled by the anxiety that rumors and disinformation create. All it does is dampen creativity and divert attention away from what matters. At first glance, the text's assertion that "the harmful effect of gossiping is believing in wrong ideas and unrealistic situations" seems too academic. We altered it to "lost in the labyrinth of rumors" to create a more striking image. The best way to end rumors and get everyone back on the same page is to have an open culture and communicate openly. Here's how to shatter the illusion and navigate the maelstrom of misinformation:

a. The Misconception Vortex: Fact vs Fiction

Competitors may quickly begin disseminating false information, such as rumors, to undermine confidence in the company. This is just an old scare tactic—stay out of this terrifying vortex. Quiet their inner voices instead. Stand out as an example of honesty and openness when it comes to sharing the undeniable worth of your service or product. If rumors start circulating regarding the stability of your company, for example, you should respond by providing them with facts and financial data.

b. The Reality Check: Facing Your Fears Head-On

One powerful cause of people's discouragement of taking risks is the fear of failing. Conversely, there is no more cancerous kind of anxiety than gossiping. Take action to find a cure. Be free from the paralysis of "what-ifs." Stay committed to your objectives and the techniques you've laid out; prepare for the unexpected by creating a contingency plan. The darkness of uncertainty will give way to the brightness of proactive readiness as you move forward with genuine steps.

c. The Power of Open Dialogue: Sunlight is the Best Disinfectant

Make sure you encourage your team members to freely interact with one another. By fostering an atmosphere of trust and open communication, we can eliminate the potential for rumors to spread and create a more cooperative workplace. According to the text, "making an open discussion to adapt to new ideas and relieve oneself from pressure" can be seen as ungainly. The aphorism "sunlight is the best disinfectant" was added to emphasize transparency and provide an aphorismatic touch.

d. The Knowledge Armor: Preparation is Key

When faced with ambiguity, knowledge is a potent weapon. Always be one step ahead of potential problems by keeping yourself updated on industry developments and creating a backup plan. "Acquiring knowledge and then emphasizing the worst scenarios which can form" is a pessimistic way to put it in the passage. We have rebranded it as an "armor of knowledge" to give it a better reputation.[12]

The Erosion of Vision: Losing Sight of the Horizon

This title injects a sense of mystery by hinting at the gradual loss of a once-clear vision. Here's a revision of the stages:

1. The Persistence Void: The Flickering Flame Extinguished

The Flickering Flame. Every entrepreneur starts their journey with a bright flame, full of ambition and hope. However, this flame can easily flicker and die without persistence. Temporary setbacks and challenges often lead to abandoning potentially great ventures, creating a persistent void that throttles innovation and progress.

To visualize this, consider the story of Thomas Edison. Edison's journey to invent the light bulb was fraught with over a thousand failed attempts. Had he succumbed to the persistence void, the world might have been deprived of one of the most significant inventions in history. His grit and

---

[12] By employing these strategies, you can silence the whisperers in the dark and emerge from the maelstrom of misinformation stronger and more focused than ever. Remember, truth is your weapon, and knowledge is your shield.

resilience kept the flame of his vision alive, ultimately bringing it to life.

Another example is Netflix's early struggles. Initially a DVD rental service, Netflix faced significant challenges, including competition from Blockbuster and skepticism about its business model. Despite these obstacles, Reed Hastings and Marc Randolph persisted. They pivoted towards streaming services, revolutionizing the entertainment industry. Their persistent vision transformed Netflix from a struggling startup into a global entertainment giant.

The flickering flame metaphor underscores the importance of developing grit and resilience. Visionaries must nurture their inner fire, keeping it alive through the highs and lows of their journey. The story of J.K. Rowling, who persisted through numerous rejections before Harry Potter became a global phenomenon, further illustrates this point. Her resilience in the face of adversity ensured her vision came to life.

These examples highlight the necessity of persistence in bringing visionary ideas to fruition. By avoiding the persistence void and continually stoking the flames of their vision, entrepreneurs can navigate through temporary setbacks and achieve enduring success.

2. The Doubtful Gaze: Failing to See the Rising Stars

The Unseen Giants. A visionary leader possesses the remarkable ability to recognize untapped potential in people. Yet, a doubtful gaze on rising talent often leads to missed opportunities and stifled innovation. Instead of focusing on the "lack of faith in new entrepreneurs," we highlight the importance of recognizing "rising stars" to emphasize the element of potential recognition.

Consider the story of Howard Schultz and Starbucks. When Schultz first proposed expanding Starbucks beyond coffee beans to serve brewed coffee, his ideas were met with skepticism. Despite the doubts, he persisted and eventually transformed Starbucks into a global coffeehouse chain, proving that recognizing and nurturing visionary ideas can lead to monumental success.

Another example is Sheryl Sandberg's role at Facebook. Mark Zuckerberg's decision to bring Sandberg on board as COO was a strategic move to harness her potential. Her leadership and vision played a crucial role in scaling Facebook's business operations, turning it into the social media giant it is today. This highlights the importance of empowering rising stars and leveraging their unique talents.

Mentorship and empowerment are key to fostering an environment where transformative ideas can flourish. Look at Google's approach to innovation. The company encourages employees to spend a portion of their time on projects they're passionate about, leading to groundbreaking products like Gmail and Google Maps. By creating a culture that values and nurtures potential, Google continues to push the boundaries of innovation.

Think of Phil Jackson's coaching style with the Chicago Bulls and the Los Angeles Lakers in sports. Jackson recognized the unique talents of players like Michael Jordan and Kobe Bryant, creating an atmosphere where they could thrive. His leadership brought out the best in these athletes and led to multiple championships, showcasing the power of seeing and nurturing rising stars.

These examples demonstrate that visionary leaders must develop the ability to see beyond the immediate and recognize the unseen giants within their teams. They can unleash transformative ideas and drive innovation to new heights by fostering mentorship and empowerment.

3. The Comfort Zone Trap: The Siren Song of Stagnation

The Security Illusion. The comfort zone may feel like a warm embrace, but it can be a prison to your dreams. Preference for security over calculated risks results in stagnation and erosion of creative vision.

Staying within the comfort zone can lead to a false sense of security, stifling growth and innovation. For example, consider Kodak, a once-dominant player in the photography industry. The company's reluctance to embrace digital technology and insistence on traditional film ultimately led to its downfall. Kodak's adherence to its comfort zone prevented it from adapting to changing market dynamics, showcasing the dangers of stagnation.

Conversely, embracing challenges and moving out of the comfort zone can lead to incredible growth and opportunities. A prime example is Netflix's pivot from DVD rentals to streaming services. This bold move involved significant risk, but it propelled the company to new heights, transforming the entertainment industry and positioning Netflix as a leader in the digital era.

Personal growth stories also illustrate this point. Take the journey of Oprah Winfrey, who stepped out of her comfort zone by taking on challenging projects and roles beyond her established TV career. Her willingness to embrace new ventures, including starting her own network and production company, has solidified her legacy as a media mogul and influential figure.

These examples highlight that while the comfort zone may offer short-term safety, true progress requires stepping into the unknown. Challenges bring new possibilities and keep your vision alive. Entrepreneurs must recognize the siren song of stagnation and choose the path of calculated risks to drive innovation and long-term success.

Causes of Deprivation of Creative Vision from People and Civilizations

Creative vision is the lifeblood of progress, a force that drives innovation and advancement. When this vision is stifled, it can cripple both individuals and civilizations, leading to stagnation and decline. Understanding the factors that deprive people and societies of creative vision is essential to fostering an environment where imagination and ingenuity can thrive. Here are some key elements that can suppress creative vision and inhibit growth:

1. Clipped Wings: The Shackles of Initiative

Stripping Personal Initiative. Think of a bird with clipped wings. This is what becomes of creative vision when personal initiative is stripped away. The freedom to act independently and explore new ideas is crucial for creativity to flourish. Bureaucracy, oppressive regimes, social pressures, and other restrictive environments can all cripple one's motivation to take risks and pursue unconventional ideas, stifling both creative outlets and innovation.

Consider the historical context of the Soviet Union. Many artists, writers, and scientists found their creative expressions severely limited during the era of intense governmental control and censorship. The suppression of dissenting ideas and strict control over intellectual pursuits stifled innovation. For instance, the work of dissident writer Aleksandr Solzhenitsyn, who dared to criticize the government, was suppressed, and he was exiled for his writings that shed light on the harsh realities of the Soviet regime. This represents a clear example of how bureaucracy and oppressive regimes can clip the wings of creative vision.

On the other hand, the United States flourished due to the spirit of personal initiative embodied by its founding fathers. The drive to explore, innovate, and build was central to the country's development. The freedom to act on new ideas without oppressive constraints enabled significant advancements in various fields. For example, Thomas Jefferson's contributions to the drafting of the Declaration of Independence and his efforts in establishing the University of Virginia reflect how personal initiative can lead to monumental progress.

Consider Silicon Valley's entrepreneurial culture in recent times. The region's success is largely attributed to an environment encouraging personal initiative, risk-taking, and innovation. Companies like Google, Apple, and Facebook were born out of this culture, where individuals could pursue their visionary ideas. The absence of stifling bureaucracy and the promotion of creative freedom have been key factors in the region's technological advancements.[13]

2. The Entitlement Maze: Lost in the Illusion of Reward

Expectations Unearned. Even in societies that value freedom and enterprise, a psychological trap can lure the

---

[13] Imagine a world painted in shades of conformity, where individuality is a forgotten whisper. This is the chilling reality for those deprived of personal initiative. The privilege to act independently and explore new ideas becomes a distant dream. Bureaucracy transforms into an impenetrable maze, and oppressive regimes cast a shadow of fear. Social pressures mutate into suffocating expectations, squeezing the very breath from creative expression.

unwary—the entitlement maze. People become lost in a labyrinth of illusion, mistaking privilege for something that is their due. They come to expect rewards without the sweat of labor and believe that effort is optional and success a birthright. This confusion between what is earned and what is imagined cripples creative vision.

The mystery deepens as one contemplates the root of this entitlement mentality. Has liberty been misconstrued, or is this just another example of an increasing trend toward instant gratification in our society? Consider the phenomenon of "participation trophies." While well-intentioned to encourage all children, they can sometimes foster an entitlement mentality, where effort and merit are undervalued. This can lead to a lack of motivation to strive for genuine achievement.

Psychologically, this belief breeds a crippling sense of helplessness when desired rewards fail to materialize. Innovation grinds to a halt, replaced by feelings of victimhood and resentment. The rise of social media has exacerbated this, with platforms often showcasing the seemingly effortless success of others, fostering unrealistic expectations and a sense of entitlement.

In the business world, the dot-com bubble of the late 1990s serves as a cautionary tale. Many tech startups, driven by the entitlement mentality of rapid success with minimal effort, collapsed when the bubble burst. Investors and entrepreneurs alike were entangled in the illusion of quick rewards, ultimately facing harsh reality checks when those expectations were unmet.

In contrast, consider the story of professional athletes like Michael Jordan. Despite immense natural talent, Jordan's success was driven by relentless hard work and dedication. His achievements were not taken for granted but earned through countless hours of practice and an unwavering commitment to excellence. This underscores the importance of effort and perseverance in achieving true success.

These examples highlight the dangers of the entitlement maze. To foster creative vision and innovation, it is essential to emphasize the value of hard work, perseverance, and earned rewards. Societies and individuals must navigate the illusion of entitlement and cultivate a mindset recognizing the necessity of effort and dedication for true achievement.

3. Capped Potential: The Labyrinth of Limited Rewards

Capping the Sky. Some employers weave an infinite net of artificial limits on earnings and opportunities. These invisible chains strangle motivation and stifle creative vision. Individuals cannot soar creatively when their rewards are artificially capped.

The mystery lies in why many organizations fear liberating their workforce's potential. Is it a jealous guarding of power or a fundamental distrust of human potential? Psychologically, these limits breed resentment and a debilitating sense of futility. Why challenge imposed constraints if there are no benefits at the prize-giving end?

Consider the example of Nokia. Once a dominant mobile phone industry, Nokia's rigid internal structure and resistance to new ideas led to its downfall. By stifling the creative potential of its employees and failing to adapt to the rapidly changing market, Nokia lost its competitive edge. This illustrates how capping potential can cripple innovation and lead to decline.

In contrast, companies like Google thrive by fostering a culture of collaboration and rewarding creativity. Google's "20% time" policy, allowing employees to spend a portion of their time on passion projects, has created groundbreaking products like Gmail and Google News. By valuing and rewarding innovative ideas, Google continuously attracts top talent and pushes the boundaries of technological advancement.

Pixar's example is also illustrative. The company's unique approach to creativity, emphasizing collaboration and open communication, has resulted in many successful films. Pixar's brain trust meetings encourage honest feedback and creative freedom, enabling the team to overcome challenges and produce innovative content.

Real success is not something to be hoarded for oneself. It matures in a tangle of shared success. Companies that fan collaboration and reward efforts and ideas will always attract the best people. Many companies that have stifled the potential of their workforces litter the annals of history, while those that enable them often blaze the trail of innovation.

These examples underscore the importance of removing artificial limits and fostering an environment where creativity can thrive. By liberating the potential of their workforce, organizations can harness the power of shared success and drive sustainable innovation.

4. The Detour of Mediocrity: The Forgotten Extra Mile

Neglecting the Extra Mile. The road to greatness is often unclear, with vague, constantly changing milestones that are hard to define. When the concept of going the "extra mile" fades from view, individuals can find themselves lost in a maze of mediocrity. Complacency is a siren, drawing one closer to a comfort zone where ambition gradually erodes. The flicker of creative desire dies, leaving only a shadow of what could have been.

History is replete with examples of individuals who began with immense potential but fizzled out along the way. The psychological blow of abandoning that extra mile is profound, resulting in a person festering in regret and a growing sense of powerlessness. This critical question begs for assessing the internal struggles or external forces that make individuals relinquish their dreams and settle for mere ordinariness.

Consider the case of Blockbuster, a company that dominated the video rental market. Despite having the resources and opportunities to innovate, Blockbuster failed to adapt to the digital age. Their reluctance to go the extra mile and explore new business models, as Netflix did, led to their downfall. This highlights how complacency and a failure to push beyond the comfort zone can lead to missed opportunities and eventual decline.

On a personal level, the story of J.K. Rowling's perseverance in the face of numerous rejections before the success of Harry Potter is an inspiring contrast. Her determination to go the extra mile despite the odds showcases the power of persistence. Her remarkable contributions to literature would have remained unrealized if she had given up.

The concept of the extra mile is also evident in sports. Michael Jordan, widely regarded as one of the greatest basketball players of all time, famously stated, "I've failed over and over and over again in my life. And that is why I succeed." Jordan's relentless work ethic and willingness to push beyond his limits exemplify the importance of going the extra mile. His dedication not only led to personal success but also inspired countless others.

These examples underscore the importance of maintaining ambition and pushing beyond the ordinary. By recognizing the allure of the comfort zone and actively choosing to challenge oneself, individuals can avoid the detour of mediocrity and achieve greatness. Embracing the extra mile is essential for keeping the flame of creative vision alive and reaching one's full potential.

5. The Mirage of Success: The Poisoned Chalice

Success's Deceptive Allure. Success is an attractive word adorned with glittering intentions yet hiding deceptive truths. Like the mirage of a desert traveler, illusory success can envelop a person, with the "poison of success" confusing knowledge with action. Those intoxicated by the fumes of past achievements often believe they are entitled to rewards merely by knowing. This hallucination cripples the drive to continually learn, innovate, and push boundaries.

Consider the story of Blackberry. Once a leader in the smartphone market, Blackberry rested on its laurels, believing its initial success would sustain it. However, this complacency led to its downfall as competitors like Apple and Samsung innovated and captured the market. Blackberry's failure to renew its creative vision and adapt highlights the dangers of being lulled by past success.

Another example is Blockbuster, which dominated the video rental market but failed to anticipate the shift to digital streaming. Despite having opportunities to innovate and evolve, Blockbuster clung to its traditional model, ultimately leading to its demise. In contrast, Netflix, which started as a DVD rental service, recognized the need for continuous innovation and transformed into a streaming giant.

On a personal level, Lance Armstrong's story serves as a cautionary tale. His early success in cycling led him to believe he was invincible, resulting in a doping scandal that shattered his career. Armstrong's reliance on past victories and refusal to adapt to ethical standards exemplify the poisoned chalice of success.

True success is a journey, not a destination. It requires constant renewal of creative vision and relentless efforts to stay ahead. Entrepreneurs and innovators must recognize that past achievements do not guarantee future success. They must remain vigilant, continuously learning and adapting to maintain their edge.

The lesson is clear: don't be seduced by the glitter of past successes. Instead, keep striving for new heights, pushing the envelope, and embracing the journey of continuous improvement and innovation.[14]

6. The Hunger that Fades: Apathy in the Garden of Plenty

The Curse of Plenty. Societies rich in wealth can become hostages of a psychological paradox: the decline of hunger. When basic needs are too readily gratified, the drive for personal achievement and self-actualization may wither. Pioneers of such societies witness inhabitants in a golden cage, content yet stagnant.

This phenomenon illustrates a crucial point: the hunger for self-determination generates creative vision. Without it, societies risk degenerating into apathy-laden twilight zones. The subtle shift from ambitious strivers to content observers is a riddle entwined in abundance. Abundance has the potential

---

[14] The mystery deepens as we consider the psychological factors at play. Success can breed arrogance and a distorted sense of entitlement. The individual becomes a locked room, hoarding their knowledge jealously instead of sharing it to fuel further creativity. The once vibrant wellspring of creative vision stagnates into a murky swamp of self-satisfaction.

to breed entitlement and detach people from the struggles that shaped previous generations.

Consider the Roman Empire in its later years. As wealth and luxury became more accessible, the Roman elite grew complacent, focusing more on indulgence than innovation. This apathy contributed to the empire's decline as the drive that once fueled expansion and progress waned.

In contrast, the early pioneers of Silicon Valley were driven by a hunger to innovate and disrupt the status quo. Despite initial setbacks and limited resources, their relentless pursuit of self-determination led to revolutionary technological advancements. The founding of companies like Apple and Hewlett-Packard in garages, driven by a passion for innovation, underscores the importance of maintaining hunger despite adversity.

Modern examples also illustrate this paradox. Countries with high living standards, like Japan and Sweden, often face challenges in maintaining high levels of ambition and innovation among their youth. Efforts to reignite the entrepreneurial spirit involve creating environments that challenge individuals and provide opportunities for self-actualization.

Elon Musk's story exemplifies hunger's power in driving creative vision. Despite his wealth, Musk continues to pursue ambitious goals like colonizing Mars and revolutionizing energy storage. His insatiable hunger for innovation keeps him pushing the boundaries, showcasing the impact of maintaining drive even in the garden of plenty.

These examples highlight the delicate balance between abundance and motivation. Societies and individuals must cultivate environments that challenge and inspire continuous growth. By recognizing the potential pitfalls of plenty, they can avoid the apathy that threatens to erode creative vision and drive.

7. The Sleeping Giant: The Indolence Enigma

Indolence's Lullaby. In the face of overabundance, complacency can set in, and a more sinister foe may emerge: indolence. With their basic needs already taken care of, people can be lulled into a psychological sleep, losing the drive to push themselves and forge new ideas. The once ardent pioneering spirit becomes just an echo of its former self, hidden away in the recesses of the mind.

Societies are often baffled by this mystery of indolence. Why should abundance, a supposed boon, breed such apathy? The answer may lie in a weakening of the survival instinct. Without the ever-present pressure to innovate and adapt, the creative muscle weakens, and the once vibrant tapestry of ideas becomes faded and threadbare.

Consider the example of the Ottoman Empire in its later years. Once a powerhouse of innovation and expansion, the empire grew complacent and indolent as it accumulated wealth and power. The lack of external pressure and internal motivation led to declining innovation and progress, contributing to the empire's eventual stagnation and downfall.

Similarly, in modern times, Japan faced a period of economic stagnation known as the "Lost Decade" during the 1990s. Despite its earlier rapid economic growth, the country's overabundance led to complacency and a decline in the drive for innovation. This period of indolence hindered Japan's economic progress, showing how abundance can sometimes lead to a lull in creative endeavors.

On an individual level, Michael Jackson's story serves as a poignant illustration. Jackson, one of the most successful artists in history, faced periods of personal and creative stagnation despite his immense wealth and fame. His struggles with indolence, amid his significant accomplishments, highlight the challenge of maintaining creative drive in the face of abundance.

These examples emphasize the need to continually challenge oneself and seek new horizons, even in times of plenty. Societies and individuals must recognize the potential dangers of indolence and strive to keep their creative muscles active. Embracing challenges and nurturing a pioneering spirit is essential to preventing the atrophy of innovation and maintaining a vibrant, forward-moving vision.

8. The Broken Equation: When Reward Loses Meaning

The Cosmic Equation. A warning: denial of the cause-and-effect relationship between contribution and reward paves the way to civilizational decline. Societies function on an unwritten equation: effort equals reward. The incentive to excel withers when that equation is broken.

The psychology of such imbalanced reward systems is devastating. If hard work does not guarantee recognition and consequent betterment, a sense of hopelessness pervades society. What was once a vibrant tapestry of creative endeavor becomes faded and threadbare, giving way to a culture of mediocrity.

Consider the fall of the Soviet Union, where the lack of a direct correlation between effort and reward stifled motivation and innovation. The rigid state-controlled system failed to incentivize individual excellence, leading to widespread inefficiency and stagnation. The breakdown of this cosmic equation ultimately contributed to the collapse of the Soviet economy.

Another example is the educational system in some countries, where grade inflation and lack of merit-based rewards can demotivate students. When students see their hard work not being adequately recognized or rewarded, their drive to excel diminishes. This leads to a broader cultural issue where mediocrity is accepted, and the pursuit of excellence wanes.

On the other hand, consider the rise of meritocratic systems like those in Finland's education system. Finland emphasizes equal opportunity and rewards effort and achievement. As a result, Finnish students consistently perform well in international assessments, and the country fosters a culture of learning and innovation. The clear link between effort and reward motivates students to strive for excellence.

In the business world, companies like Salesforce have implemented innovative reward systems to maintain high levels of employee motivation. By recognizing and rewarding individual contributions through bonuses, promotions, and public acknowledgment, Salesforce cultivates a culture of excellence and continuous improvement.

The trick is to design a system that balances individual freedom with incentives to innovate. Societies must foster environments where intrinsic motivation thrives alongside opportunities for extrinsic reward. Only then does creative vision have any chance to blossom.[15]

9. **The Sterile Soil: The Paradox of Forced Contribution.**

    Bound by Dictators, forced service can be injurious to creative vision. Societal advancement necessitates contribution, but for it to be effective, it must come by choice. Laws and regulations

---

[15] By understanding these obstacles, we can work to create environments that nurture creative vision. This includes encouraging personal initiative, rewarding effort and innovation, and fostering a culture of continuous learning and growth. Only then can individuals and civilizations reach their full potential.

that stifle initiative and hamper innovation ultimately cultivate the seeds of sterility in the garden of creativity. These iron shackles snuff out the intrinsic motivation that fuels novel ideas.

Consider the example of state-mandated art in totalitarian regimes. In the Soviet Union, Socialist Realism was imposed as the official artistic style, limiting artists to producing works that conformed to state propaganda. This stifling of artistic freedom led to a lack of genuine creativity and innovation. The artists were turned into automatons, their work driven by obligation rather than passion. While technically proficient, the resulting art lacked the vitality and originality stemming from true creative freedom.

In contrast, the flourishing of creativity during the Renaissance highlights the power of voluntary contribution. The patronage system allowed artists to explore their visions freely, resulting in an explosion of innovation and masterpieces that continue to inspire generations. The support of patrons like the Medici family enabled artists like Leonardo da Vinci and Michelangelo to pursue their creative passions, unburdened by oppressive dictates.

The psychological effects of coerced creativity are paralyzing. When people become mere automatons, their actions are no longer driven by the passion that sparks innovation. Resentment embeds itself at the base of the creative well, poisoning it and replacing its source with obligation and drudgery. The story of Franz Kafka, who worked in an insurance office while writing his seminal works in his spare time, underscores this point. Kafka's creative output was driven by his passion for writing, not by the demands of his day job, illustrating the difference between voluntary and forced contribution.

In modern workplaces, companies that foster voluntary contributions and encourage employees to pursue their creative ideas often see greater innovation and job satisfaction. Google's 20% time policy is a prime example, where employees are given the freedom to work on projects they are passionate about, leading to breakthroughs like Gmail and AdSense.

These examples highlight the importance of fostering an environment where voluntary contributions are driven by genuine interest. Societies and organizations must recognize the detrimental effects of forced contribution and cultivate a culture that values and nurtures intrinsic motivation for true creative flourishing.

10. The Rude Awakening: The Crucible of Crisis

That's a dark truth, but at times, a rude awakening shatters the illusions that unprepared creativity remains. This awakening often comes through catastrophe, a crucible of crisis that forces societies to reassess their priorities. Depression or war may strip away the comforts of abundance, leaving the basic imperatives of human ingenuity and effort laid bare.

The question arises: must a society be brought to its knees before rediscovering its creative energies? Crisis generates a profound psychic impact. Despair may cripple a society, but it can also drive people to desperate ingenuity, giving them a fighting chance of survival.

Consider the Great Depression in the United States. The economic collapse forced countless individuals and companies to innovate just to survive. President Franklin D. Roosevelt's New Deal introduced sweeping reforms and public works projects that spurred innovation and economic recovery. This crisis period reshaped American society and underscored the potential for innovation born from necessity.

World War II provides another example. The war effort required unprecedented levels of innovation and collaboration, leading to advancements in technology, medicine, and industry. The urgent demands of the war accelerated the development of radar, the first computers, and medical breakthroughs like penicillin. The crisis forced societies to push the boundaries of their capabilities, resulting in lasting advancements.

In recent times, the COVID-19 pandemic has served as a modern crucible of crisis. The pandemic disrupted economies and daily life, spurring rapid innovation in healthcare, remote work technology, and digital communication. Companies and individuals adapted swiftly, finding new ways to connect, work, and provide services. This period highlighted the resilience and adaptability of human ingenuity in the face of global challenges.

The hope lies in learning from past errors and cultivating a culture of innovation during periods of peace and prosperity. Societies must strive to harness the creative energy that often emerges in crisis without waiting for catastrophe to strike. We can maintain our creative vision and be better prepared for future challenges by fostering an environment that encourages continuous innovation and learning.

11. Fleeting Fancies: Lost in the Mental Wind

Fleeting thoughts and mere wishes are like fallen leaves— dispersed, undetected, and swiftly forgotten by the subconscious mind. They lack the weight and conviction required to create an indelible impression. The subconscious craves concentrated resolve and the tireless pursuit of well-defined desires. Stray ideas and half-hearted hopes are carried away like whispers in a vast abyss, leaving no permanent mark.

Consider the world of inventors and visionaries. Thomas Edison famously said, "Genius is one percent inspiration, ninety-nine percent perspiration." His success was not just a product of fleeting ideas but of relentless determination and focused effort. Edison's tireless pursuit and single-minded resolve turned his ideas into reality, showcasing the importance of persistence in nurturing creative vision.

Similarly, the story of J.K. Rowling's journey to publish the Harry Potter series exemplifies the power of unwavering determination. Despite facing numerous rejections, Rowling's concentrated resolve and tireless effort eventually led to one of history's most successful literary franchises. Her well-defined desire to tell her story kept her going through adversity, turning fleeting fancies into a lasting legacy.

In the realm of technology, Steve Jobs' vision for Apple was not a product of sporadic thoughts but a relentless focus on creating revolutionary products. Jobs' ability to concentrate his efforts on well-defined goals resulted in groundbreaking innovations like the iPhone and Mac, transforming entire industries.

The mind requires constant attention, intensity, and determination to achieve a specific objective. Without this, dispersed thoughts are whisked away by the winds of the mind, never to be planted in the fruitful ground of creation. Visionaries who succeed harness their fleeting ideas, nurture them with unwavering dedication and pursue them with relentless effort.

These examples illustrate that while fleeting fancies may spark creativity, concentrated resolve, and tireless pursuit ultimately bring those ideas to life. Individuals can turn their ephemeral thoughts into enduring contributions by maintaining focused attention and determination.[16]

---

[16] "Shadows of the Mind" explores how environmental factors and the brain's auto-acquisition processes serve as the foundation for the generation of thoughts. The book emphasizes that the environmental factors and auto-acquisition of processes by the human brain are the basis of mind thought generation.

EPILOGUE

ઠેઠેઠે

This part showed the basic shift that needs to take place to awaken success consciousness. We went beyond the simple pursuit of wealth and looked into the significance of serving, contributing, and creating something of value. This chapter focused on the critical psychological attributes of success: tenacity, adaptability, and self-belief, couching them as the entrepreneur's philosopher's stone. We followed this up with some threats that have hijacked your startup: quick riches illusion, unethical shortcuts, and erosion of vision. Understanding these psychological traps will enable entrepreneurs to navigate them and emerge as winners.

Important Remarks:

- **Success is a journey, not a destination.** It's something you obsess over the creative process and what you give to the world.

- **Develop an unwavering belief in yourself and your vision.** This inner fire will fuel your persistence in the face of challenges.

- **Build strong relationships and act with integrity.** Your success is intertwined with the success of those around you.

- **Embrace a growth mindset.** Be willing to adapt and learn from your experiences.

Remember, the entrepreneur's path is paved with both triumph and tribulation. By cultivating success consciousness, you equip yourself with the psychological tools to navigate the labyrinth and emerge victorious. Onward, to the next chapter of your entrepreneurial adventure!

SECOND BOOK: THE EVOLUTION OF THOUGHT

The Symphony of Thought Unraveling the Enigma: A Journey Through the Mind's Symphony

❧ ❧ ❧

P repare to be enthralled by the enigmatic journey that awaits you as you delve into the labyrinthine depths of the human mind. In this investigation, we will venture into the enigmatic workings that control our thoughts, uncovering the concealed patterns that influence our views, convictions, and behaviors.

This adventure will lead us through the intricate maze of the CgX system, a mesmerizing web of interconnected neural pathways that shape our thoughts and actions. We will explore the complex interplay between nature and nurture, delving into the depths of human consciousness.

Together, we will embark on a journey to unravel the enigmatic depths of the human mind as it orchestrates the intricate melodies that compose the tapestry of our existence. We will explore the enigmatic realm of unlocking hidden potential, transcending societal expectations, and crafting a personal symphony that resonates with purpose, balance, and satisfaction.

Get ready to be captivated by the intricate melodies of the mind as we embark on an extraordinary adventure of self-discovery and transformation.

www.ingramcontent.com/pod-product-compliance
Lightning Source LLC
Chambersburg PA
CBHW061150120626
46546CB00005B/1994